DATE DUE		
4-14-98		
4-27-98		
MR 19 03		

947
BAC

Bachrach, Deborah.

**The Charge of the
Light Brigade**

652805 02155   00028D   004

The Charge of the Light Brigade

Books in the Battles Series:

The Attack on Pearl Harbor

The Battle of Antietam

The Battle of Belleau Wood

The Battle of Britain

The Battle of Gettysburg

The Battle of Hastings

The Battle of Marathon

The Battle of Midway

The Battle of Stalingrad

The Battle of Waterloo

The Battle of Zama

The Charge of the Light Brigade

Defeat of the Spanish Armada

The Inchon Invasion

The Invasion of Normandy

The Tet Offensive

✣ Battles of the Nineteenth Century ✣

The Charge of the Light Brigade

by Deborah Bachrach

Lucent Books, P.O. Box 289011, San Diego, CA 92198-9011

For Josef Altholz,
my teacher and friend

Library of Congress Cataloging-in-Publication Data

Bachrach, Deborah, 1943–
    The Charge of the Light Brigade / by Deborah Bachrach.
      p. cm. — (Battles of the nineteenth century)
    Includes bibliographical references and index.
    Summary: Examines the Charge of the Light Brigade within
the context of the Battle of Balaclava.
    ISBN 1-56006-455-2 (alk. paper)
    1. Balaklava (Ukraine), Battle of, 1854—Juvenile literature.
[1. Balaklava (Ukraine), Battle of, 1854. 2. Crimean War, 1853–1856.]
I. Title. II. Series.
DK215.3.B33 1997
947'.073—dc20   96-21505
                                                                      CIP
                                                                      AC

Printed in the U.S.A.

Copyright 1997 by Lucent Books, Inc., P.O. Box 289011,
San Diego, CA 92198-9011

Contents

Foreword

Almost everyone would agree with William Tecumseh Sherman that war "is all hell." Yet the history of war, and battles in particular, is so fraught with the full spectrum of human emotion and action that it becomes a microcosm of the human experience. Soldiers' lives are condensed and crystallized in a single battle. As Francis Miller explains in his *Photographic History of the Civil War* when describing the war wounded, "It is sudden, the transition from marching bravely at morning on two sound legs, grasping your rifle in two sturdy arms, to lying at nightfall under a tree with a member forever gone."

Decisions made on the battlefield can mean the lives of thousands. A general's pique or indigestion can result in the difference between life and death. Some historians speculate, for example, that Napoleon's fateful defeat at Waterloo was due to the beginnings of stomach cancer. His stomach pain may have been the reason that the normally decisive general was sluggish and reluctant to move his troops. And what kept George McClellan from winning battles during the Civil War? Some scholars and contemporaries believe that it was simple cowardice and fear. Others argue that he felt a gut-wrenching unwillingness to engage in the war of attrition that was characteristic of that particular conflict.

Battle decisions can be magnificently brilliant and horribly costly. At the Battle of Thaspus in 47 B.C., for example, Julius Caesar, facing a numerically superior army, shrewdly ordered his troops onto a narrow strip of land bordering the sea. Just as he expected, his enemy thought he had accidentally trapped himself and divided their forces to surround his troops. By dividing their army, his enemy had given Caesar the strategic edge he needed to defeat them. Other battle orders result in disaster, as in the case of the Battle of Balacava during the Crimean War in 1854. A British general gave the order to attack a force of withdrawing enemy Russians. But confusion in relaying the order resulted in the 673 men of the Light Brigade's charging in the wrong direction into certain death by heavy enemy cannon fire. Battles are the stuff of history on the grandest scale—their outcomes often determine whether nations are enslaved or liberated.

Moments in battles illustrate the best and worst of human character. In the feeling of terror and the us-versus-them attitude that accompanies war, the enemy can be dehumanized and treated with a contempt that is considered repellent in times of peace. At Wounded Knee, the distrust and anticipation of violence that grew between the Native Americans and American soldiers led to the senseless killing of ninety men, women, and children. And who can forget My Lai, where the deaths of old men, women, and children at the hands of American soldiers shocked an America already disillusioned with the Vietnam War. The murder of six million Jews will remain burned into the human conscience forever as the measure of man's inhumanity to man. These horrors cannot be forgotten. And yet, under the terrible conditions of battle, one can find acts of bravery, kindness, and altruism. During the Battle of Midway, the members of Torpedo Squadron 8, flying in hopelessly antiquated planes and without the benefit of air protection from fighters, tried bravely to fulfill their mission—to destroy the *Kido Butai,* the Japanese Carrier Striking Force. Without air support, the squadron was immediately set upon by Japanese fighters. Nevertheless, each bomber tried valiantly to hit his target. Each failed. Every man but one died in the effort. But by keeping the Japanese fighters busy, the squadron bought time and delayed further Japanese fighter attacks. In the aftermath of the Battle of Isandhlwana in South Africa in 1879, a force of thousands of Zulu warriors trapped a contingent of British troops in a small trading post. After repeated bloody attacks in which many died on both sides, the Zulus, their final victory certain, granted the remaining British their lives as a gesture of respect for their bravery. During World War I, American troops were so touched by the fate of French war orphans that they took up a collection to help them. During the Civil War, soldiers of the North and South would briefly forget that they were enemies and share smokes and coffee across battle lines during the endless nights. These acts seem all the more dramatic, more uplifting, because they indicate that people can continue to behave with humanity when faced with inhumanity.

Lucent Books' Battles Series highlights the vast range of the human character revealed in the ordeal of war. Dramatic narrative describes in exciting and accurate detail the commanders, soldiers, weapons, strategies, and maneuvers involved in each battle. Each volume includes a comprehensive historical context, explaining what brought the parties to war, the events leading to the battle, what factors made the battle important, and the effects it had on the larger war and later events.

The Battles Series also includes a chronology of important dates that gives students an overview, at a glance, of each battle. Sidebars create a broader context by adding enlightening details on leaders, institutions, customs, warships, weapons, and armor mentioned in the narration. Every volume contains numerous maps that allow readers to better visualize troop movements and strategies. In addition, numerous primary and secondary source quotations drawn from both past historical witnesses and modern historians are included. These quotations demonstrate to readers how and where historians derive information about past events. Finally, the volumes in the Battles Series provide a launching point for further reading and research. Each book contains a bibliography designed for student research, as well as a second bibliography that includes the works the author consulted while compiling the book.

Above all, the Battles Series helps illustrate the words of Herodotus, the fifth-century B.C. Greek historian now known as the "father of history." In the opening lines of his great chronicle of the Greek and Persian Wars, the world's first battle book, he set for himself this goal: "To preserve the memory of the past by putting on record the astonishing achievements both of our own and of other peoples; and more particularly, to show how they came into conflict."

Chronology of Events

1854

September 14
Allies land on Crimean peninsula.

September 20
Battle of the Alma.

The Highlanders attack the Russian redoubt at the Battle of the Alma, the first victory for the allies.

September 26
British decide to use port of Balaclava as their base of supply.

October 17
Bombardment of Sebastopol begins.

October 20
Bombardment of Sebastopol fails.

October 21
Turkish spies report on Russian activities.

October 24
Spies alert the British that attack will begin the following day.

October 25
5:00 A.M.   Russians begin move toward redoubts.

5:30   Lord Lucan sends warning of attack to Lord Raglan.

6:00–7:30   Russians overrun redoubts one, two, three, and four.

7:30   Surviving Turkish defenders retreat toward Balaclava.

8:45   Russian detachment begins attack on Ninety-third Regiment defending approach to Balaclava at town of Kadikoi.

9:00   Ninety-third Highlanders defend position and Russians retreat.

9:05   Main body of Russian cavalry appears over top of Causeway Heights.

9:07   Halt of Russian cavalry.

9:10   General Sir James Scarlett arranges his troops.

9:15   Charge of the Heavy Brigade.

9:23   Heavy Brigade achieves victory over Russian cavalry.

10:30   British infantry reaches the Balaclava Plain.

10:45   Raglan orders Lucan to go to the front.

10:50   Lucan conveys Raglan's message to Lord Cardigan.

10:55   Cardigan protests against nature of orders but decides to obey; misinterprets orders and charges in wrong direction.

The ill-fated Charge of the Light Brigade, a disastrous mistake for the British.

11:00   Charge of the Light Brigade.

11:05   French attack Russians on Fedioukine Hills.

11:10   French take the Russian guns on the Fedioukine Hills.

11:20   Return of the remnants of the Light Brigade.

INTRODUCTION

The Valley of Death

The famous Charge of the Light Brigade was part of the action of the Battle of Balaclava, one of the earlier and most important battles of the Crimean War. Fought largely between the armies of Russia and Britain, it took place near the approaches to the south Crimean port of Balaclava during the morning hours of October 25, 1854.

Eventually, the Crimean War pitted the armies of Britain, France, Turkey, and Sardinia against Russia. The main objective of the allied armies was to capture and destroy the massive Russian naval base Sebastopol. By destroying Sebastopol, the allies would eliminate an enormous arsenal and the home base to a large and powerful Russian fleet.

Because Sebastopol is situated on the west coast of the Crimean peninsula, which juts into the Black Sea, Russia was able to control the Black Sea. Russia was able to gain access to the countries along the sea and the important European waterways, such as the Danube, that emptied into it. Then, in the early 1850s, Russia began efforts to gain control of the countries that border the shores of the Black Sea, including Turkey. Russia was interested in Turkey because it also lay astride an important body of water called the Straits. The Straits connect the Black Sea and the Mediterranean Sea. Because the Black Sea is an enclosed body of water, gaining control of Turkey and the Straits would give Russia a route for its warships to enter the Mediterranean Sea.

Britain and France wanted to prevent Russia from obtaining a route to the Mediterranean Sea because Russia could maneuver

The Crimean Peninsula

its navy to threaten British and French bases located around its shores. In addition, Britain, France, and Sardinia had important financial and political interests in Turkey and in the Mediterranean Sea. In order to prevent Russia from obtaining entry to Turkey, the British, French, and Sardinian governments decided to invade Russia through the Crimean peninsula and to destroy Sebastopol.

The allied invasion ships sailed from the Mediterranean Sea, through the Straits and into the Black Sea to Russia. The British established their base of supply at the small port of Balaclava on the southern coast of the Crimean peninsula, about six miles from Sebastopol. The security of this base was critical to the British war effort. Military supplies, food, and clothing arrived by ship at Balaclava for distribution to the British army encamped near the Russian fortifications that guarded the approaches to Sebastopol.

The Russian High Command understood the importance of Balaclava to the British war effort. The Russians also saw the British as the leading member of the coalition arrayed against them. Russia wanted to dislodge Britain from its port and force it to withdraw from the war in the hopes that the other allies would also withdraw. Then the invasion of Russia would end before the onset of the dreaded Russian winter. The stage was set: The allies aimed to destroy Sebastopol, and the Russian High Command wanted to destroy the British position at Balaclava and drive them out of the war.

Four separate actions took place on October 25, 1854. The four taken together compose the Battle of Balaclava. All but the last, the Charge of the Light Brigade, are largely omitted in general histories of the period.

The relative neglect of these other phases of the battle is curious. Had it not been for the Charge of the Light Brigade, the last of the four actions, the British could have considered the overall battle a victory. While the Turks failed to hold their position during the first phase of the battle, the British were very successful in the second and third actions. In phases two and three of the Battle of Balaclava, British military units fought bravely and audaciously, successfully turning back formidable Russian cavalry units. As a result of the Charge of the Light Brigade, however, the Russians likely could have driven the British from Balaclava if they had taken advantage of the loss of most of the British cavalry.

Ineffective communication by the British leaders, internal staff animosities, inadequate planning, administrative ineptitude, and an almost criminal lack of professional military leadership all took their terrible toll. These factors led to one of the most disastrous and unnecessary cavalry charges in modern history. More than six hundred men and horses charged in the wrong direction. British troops rushed against vastly superior Russian units aided by powerful field guns and an overwhelmingly superior tactical position on the field of battle. Bravery, blind loyalty to

British troops, hampered by internal miscommunication and inexperienced officers, are slaughtered by the Russians during the Charge of the Light Brigade.

the traditions of military units, and dedication to queen and country on the part of the British soldiers all proved inadequate to avert catastrophe.

The charge was a failure. The Light Brigade was destroyed as a fighting unit. Ironically, however, the pitiful and useless morning's slaughter of men and horses in "the valley of death" came to symbolize all that was great in the British military tradition. Alfred Lord Tennyson, the British poet, for example, almost immediately immortalized the actions of the troopers of the Light Brigade in his poem "The Charge of the Light Brigade." Generations remembered the glory of the charge, not the gore and failure.

The British people held to Tennyson's interpretation of the battle because of the great value they placed on unquestioning loyalty to tradition and country, even in the face of clear and impending disaster. These values stemmed from the military customs and mores of the victorious armies of the duke of Wellington a half century earlier. The great duke did not die until 1852, and the continuation of his military thinking was almost an article of faith in Britain.

In those armies ordinary soldiers were treated merely as cannon fodder. They were sacrificed to the whims of their aristocratic officers. This long-standing military custom was a result of the great esteem in which the aristocracy was held. In addition, given the lack of inexpensive newspapers and war journalists,

Despite the devastating failure of the Light Brigade, the British people honored the charge as a glorious endeavor. Here, the queen welcomes the guards back from the Crimea at Buckingham Palace.

the general public did not know that the lives of their sons were held to be of such little value.

Tragically, these customs continued to govern British military thinking during the Crimean War. Some persisted even until the eve of World War I. The country doggedly honored its fallen heroes, admired its generals, and only very reluctantly altered the administrative shortcomings and ancient traditions that contributed to the tragic destruction of so many lives.

While posterity has telescoped the events of October 25, 1854, into a single action, the Charge of the Light Brigade, the charge itself was the last, but not the decisive, action of that bloody morning. In fact, while the Russians made considerable gains, they did not achieve their objective of driving the British out of Balaclava. The British siege of Sebastopol continued for another eighteen months.

The Russians, like the British, continued to follow the military traditions of an earlier age. Their leaders were not trained to take the initiative; instead they blindly followed the orders of their chiefs, most of whom, like the British, were untrained, unskilled, and elderly. The Russians could not take advantage of the overwhelming superiority of their forces, particularly of their large cavalry units, and let victory slip through their fingers. They failed to exploit unexpected opportunities that day, such as the almost criminal weakness of the British defenses around the port of Balaclava.

It took many years for the British people to lose their reverence for military leaders who had no military training and who treated their units as tools to further their own ambitions. Balaclava, however, did provide the British with the knowledge that reform was needed. Because Russia, unlike Britain, was an autocratic state, the government could ignore the shortcomings in its army. As a result, for the Russian common soldier, reform came painfully and tragically slowly.

The Battle of Balaclava provides a fine example of the gallantry displayed by British enlisted troops as well as the solid quality of obedience of the Russian soldiers. It also provides painful insights into the difficult task of altering long-honored national institutions and demonstrates that victory often depends on the ineptitude of the enemy rather than on the skill of the victor.

CHAPTER ONE

What Caused the Crimean War?

When historians talk about the causes of particular wars, they often discuss both the immediate and the long-term causes of the conflicts. The long-term causes of wars are deep antagonisms between groups or countries, some going back many hundreds of years. These disputes are a part of the essential history of the nations and their people.

The immediate causes of wars are the sparks—an assassination, a minor border dispute—that can occur at any time in the course of the long-term dispute. Viewed in isolation, these events might seem too insignificant to explain the conflict that follows. Sometimes, however, they occur at a moment of great turmoil or one that is ripe for upheaval. If war begins, these momentary sparks are called the immediate causes of the war.

The shots fired at Lexington and Concord, where British soldiers shot unarmed American colonists before the Revolutionary War, for example, provided the spark that ignited the long-simmering differences between the American colonists and the mother country. There had already been violent encounters between the two sides. This time, however, both the colonists and the British were willing to fight, and war followed. The result was the independence of the United States of America.

Long-Term Causes of the Crimean War

Similarly, the Crimean War had many long-term causes, but it was sparked by a seemingly remote incident. The long-term causes lay deep in the history of the major nations of Europe.

For centuries each major power had, in turn, tried to establish its dominance over the others. In the seventeenth and again in the late-eighteenth century, for example, France tried to gain control over all of Europe. Both times Britain successfully managed to prevent France from accomplishing its goal.

In the mid–nineteenth century, the Russians began to threaten the balance of power. Russia wanted to establish control not only over the Black Sea but also over the Straits that connected the Black Sea and the Mediterranean Sea. The Russians gradually increased their control over non-Russian peoples to the east and appeared ready to establish control over other lands that contained the important trade routes to India from which Britain gained much wealth. Because Turkey dominated both the Straits that led into the Mediterranean Sea and access to these overland trade routes, to achieve its goals, Russia had to take control of Turkey.

Britain's fears of an attempted invasion of Turkey intensified when the weak Turkish Empire was in danger of disintegration. Abdul Medjid, the sultan (or ruler) of the Turkish Empire was dull and ineffectual and unable to control the vast empire he had inherited. In fact, many European leaders referred to the Turkish Empire as "the sick man of Europe."

Neither Britain nor Russia wanted to see the other power gain a predominant position in Turkey following a long-expected Turkish disintegration. Both countries wanted to be prepared to act quickly in the event that the Turkish government ceased to exist, thereby causing a power vacuum in the region. Both spent large amounts of money on their respective fleets. While Russia's fleet patrolled the Black Sea, the British navy patrolled the Mediterranean Sea. Both countries wanted to be ready in the event that Turkey ceased to exist.

In such a volatile situation, any spark can set off a major crisis. That spark was provided, curiously enough, by a dispute among some monks in Palestine in 1852. Roman Catholic and Greek Orthodox monks had lived together uneasily in Palestine for many hundreds of years. Often they vied for control of the various holy shrines that were sacred to both denominations, but their squabbles had never led to war. Abdul Medjid, who ruled Palestine as well as Turkey, was a Moslem. He tolerated these disputes among the Christian groups in his empire because their fights did not threaten his own authority. When the disputes became violent, the monks usually appealed to the sultan to settle their differences.

Turkish sultan Abdul Medjid's failure to resolve a dispute between Roman Catholic and Greek Orthodox monks in Palestine ultimately led to the Crimean War.

Russian Desire to Divide Turkey with Great Britain

The tsar believed that Britain and the British government would be receptive to his ideas about dividing up the Turkish Empire. This view becomes clear from Ambassador Seymour's description of the conversation that he had with Nicholas I in 1853. The quotation is taken from Alexis S. Troubetzkoy's *The Road to Balaklava*. Nicholas is speaking:

> You know my feelings with regard to England. . . . It is essential that the two governments, that is, the English Government and I should be on the best of terms. The necessity was never greater than at present [in view of the weakness of Turkey]. I beg you to convey these words to Lord John Russell [British prime minister who succeeded Aberdeen]. When we are agreed, I am quite without anxiety as to the rest of Europe; it is quite immaterial what the other countries may think or do. We have on our hands a sick man—a very sick man. It will be a great misfortune if one of these days he should slip away from us, especially before all necessary arrangements were made. However, this is not the time to speak to you on this matter.

In 1852 yet another in a long series of disputes arose over who would control access to such holy shrines in Palestine as the Church of the Nativity, which were associated with the life of Jesus of Nazareth. The Roman Catholic and Greek Orthodox monks, each claiming control over the holy places, appealed as usual to the sultan to resolve the situation.

The dispute took on ominous overtones when it became intertwined with the far larger question of Russian territorial ambitions. The sultan vacillated for months, fearing that any decision he made regarding the dispute would anger one of the European powers. If he granted too much control to the Roman Catholic monks, he would anger the tsar but please the French. If he granted too much control to the Greek Orthodox, he would please the tsar but cause the French and British to see this as an opening for the tsar to gain still more influence over Turkish affairs. Russia, Britain, and France each gradually came to believe that the dispute would somehow affect their vital national interests. The leaders of the three countries believed that this dispute was the first step in the breakup of the Turkish Empire. None of the countries could permit such a geopolitical earthquake to occur without its interference.

Russian Involvement in Turkish Matters

Nicholas I, tsar of Russia and a member of the Greek Orthodox religion, naturally championed the cause of the Greek Orthodox monks. He claimed to be the international defender of members of the Orthodox Church wherever they lived.

In the tsar's mind, this role extended to protecting the twelve million Orthodox Christians who lived within the European part of the Turkish Empire. He expressed the fear that the sultan was mistreating his coreligionists and demanded that the weak sultan give up control over these people.

Most of the Orthodox Christians lived in south and central Europe along the shores of the Black Sea. If Nicholas made good his claim, he would effectively establish Russian control over the Black Sea region and over the Straits that led into the Mediterranean Sea.

Nicholas wanted Abdul Medjid to take the Russian demands seriously, so the tsar sent his chief minister, Prince Alexander Menshikov, to the Turkish capital, Constantinople. Menshikov arrived in a ship appropriately called the *Thunderer* to present his demands to the sultan. When the Turks turned down the tsar's demands to settle the monks' dispute in favor of the Greek Orthodox and to turn over control of the twelve million Greek Orthodox in Europe, the prince left Constantinople in a great fury. Nicholas decided to take action. On July 2, 1853, he sent his troops across the Pruth River into two European provinces of Turkey called Moldavia and Wallachia.

Russian tsar Nicholas I prepared to take over parts of the Turkish Empire under the guise of defending the Greek Orthodox religion.

Britain Enters the Dispute

The seriousness of the situation did not escape the notice of the British and the French. Great Britain, as a Protestant power, did not really care which monks controlled the keys to the Church of the Nativity in Bethlehem. However, Queen Victoria; her prime minister, Lord Aberdeen; Parliament; and the British people cared a great deal about the movement of large Russian armies into Turkish territory.

They believed that Nicholas seriously intended to take over parts of the Turkish Empire. In fact, Nicholas had been trying to get Britain to agree to such a division since the 1840s. In March 1853, Nicholas and Sir Hamilton Seymour, the British ambassador to St. Petersburg, openly discussed the possibility of destroying the Turkish Empire. Seymour immediately wrote to his superiors in London about the tsar's suggestion. According to Seymour, the tsar told him: "We have a sick man on our hands [Turkey], a man who is seriously ill; it will be a great misfortune if he escapes us one of these days, especially before all the necessary arrangements are made."

Tsar Nicholas as Religious Leader

Tsar Nicholas appealed to the religious faith of the Russian people as he prepared for war against Britain, France, and Turkey. The following passage shows how he combined that appeal with a strong military message. The quotation is taken from Constantin de Grunwald's *Tzar Nicholas I.*

> By the grace of God, we, Nicholas I, Emperor and Autocrat of all the Russians, make known to our faithful and well-beloved subjects, that from time immemorial our glorious predecessors took the vow to defend the Orthodox faith. Now, having exhausted all means of persuasion and all means of obtaining in a friendly manner the satisfaction due to our just reclamation, we have deemed it indispensable to order our troops to enter the Danubian Principalities, to show the Port [Sultan] how far its obstinacy may lead it. We do not seek conquests. Russia does not need them. We demand only satisfaction for a legitimate right infringed.

Now it appeared that Nicholas would make those arrangements on his own. The British became alarmed. They were especially concerned by the idea that Russia, already huge, would gain additional territory. In fact, for much of the nineteenth century, defending Turkey against a Russian takeover and safeguarding the Straits were key elements in British foreign policy.

The strength of this policy is indicated clearly by the following excerpt from a letter that the duke of Argyll, a member of the British House of Lords, wrote at the beginning of 1854 to an old friend:

> There is no feature in the physical geography of our globe so peculiar in its political significance as that which consists of the two channels of the Bosporus and the Dardanelles, with the Sea of Marmara [the Straits] between them.

Therefore, the British decided that they too had to demonstrate their interest in the outcome of the quarrels in Palestine. They sent their extremely influential diplomat Sir Stratford de Redcliffe to Constantinople. He consulted with the sultan and his ministers. Redcliffe's presence strengthened Abdul Medjid's decision not to relinquish his control over his own subjects. (Shortly after Redcliffe arrived, Prince Menshikov left Constantinople in a fury.)

France Enters the Dispute

France, too, entered the quarrel, claiming that historically the kings of France had defended Roman Catholic interests in the Holy Land. In fact, French entry into the crisis had little to do with this claim.

Napoleon III, emperor of France, joined the British in their fight against the Russians. However, Napoleon's motives were political rather than religious: He hoped to gain support from French Roman Catholics as well as secure a diplomatic relationship with Great Britain.

Rather, the new ruler of France, Napoleon III, nephew of the great Napoleon Bonaparte, wanted to play a more important role in European affairs. He hoped to gain the support of Roman Catholics within France by appearing to support the Roman Catholic monks in Palestine. Above all, he wanted to gain the diplomatic friendship of Great Britain.

So Napoleon III used the crisis in Palestine as an opportunity to join with Great Britain in the dispute with the Russians over the preservation of the Turkish Empire. Nicholas's invasion of Turkish territory quickly turned a dispute among a group of monks into a much more dangerous international crisis than the British or the French had anticipated.

The British and French could not back down from their stated position. Therefore, they determined to defend the current ruler of the Turkish Empire and to keep the anti-Russian Abdul Medjid in control of all of his lands.

The Importance of the Straits to Great Britain

The following quote is from a speech that the duke of Argyll made in 1854. It demonstrates how fiercely many people in Britain regarded the need to protect Turkey from Russian troops. The quotation is taken from Alexis S. Troubetzkoy's *The Road to Balaklava*.

> There is no feature in the physical geography of our globe so peculiar in its political significance as that which consists in the two channels of the Bosphorus and the Dardanelles, with the Sea of Marmara between them. Nowhere else in the world is there a vast inland sea, more than 700 miles broad, that washes the shore of two separate quarters of the world, and yet opens with a mouth as narrow as the neck of a bottle, so that the Power possessing it must have irresistible facilities of attack from a position altogether impregnable in defence. If this imperial dominion were to be added to what Russia already has, the Black Sea would be a Russian lake, the Danube would be a Russian river, and some of the richest provinces of Eastern Europe and of Western Asia would give to Russia inexhaustible resources of men, in money, and in ships. With these, together with a unique position of geographical advantage, she would possess inordinate power over the rest of Europe.

The British and French fleets sailed to the entrance of the Straits. They hoped their presence would encourage the Russians to withdraw their troops from the two Turkish provinces. Instead their presence emboldened Abdul Medjid to demand that the Russians withdraw all their troops from Turkish territory. The Russians at first refused to withdraw. The Turks then jumped the gun and, without consulting Britain and France, declared war against Russia on October 23, 1853.

None of the powers wanted to fight a major war. None was prepared to do so. Consequently, for many months the allies and the Russians tried to negotiate terms that would allow all sides to withdraw from the dispute gracefully.

While the diplomats exchanged notes, however, the Turks decided to defend their territory on their own. The sultan called up his troops, numbering over 150,000 men; to the surprise of military experts, the Turkish soldiers displayed remarkable courage in their battles against the tsar's forces.

One of these battles included a Russian attack on Silistria, a Turkish town that lies about sixty miles north of the Bulgarian port of Varna. The Turks needed to prevent the Russian army from moving south of Silistria and threatening Constantinople.

Turkish resistance to the Russian invaders was so strong that the Russian army at Silistria lifted the siege of the city and retreated

Turkish troops, without the aid of their allies, fend off Russian invaders and force them to retreat during the siege of Silistria.

toward the Russian border. The Turks also forced a Russian army retreat from a second position, at Guirgeveo, fifty miles northwest of Silistria. The Russian army under General Prince M. D. Gorchakov decided it had had enough and recrossed the Pruth River in August.

According to the historian Peter Gibbs:

> The Turks had beaten off the menace of Russian invasion without any help from the allies, other than an unofficial contribution by ten British officers and a couple of gunboats. The threat of Russian domination of the Bosporus, which had brought Britain and France into the war, had been effectively removed.

The allied leaders, both military and civilian, found themselves in an awkward situation. Their fleets were in Turkish waters, prepared to defend the sultan. After long and embarrassing delays, their armies were preparing to leave for Turkey, but the Russians had already left the field of battle.

British and French citizens, who were unaware of the situation, were decidedly pro-war. In Britain, Queen Victoria, Prince Albert, and their children proudly smiled and waved as the troops passed in review on the way to their ships. Queen Victoria wrote to her uncle, the king of Belgium, that "They formed in line, presented arms, and cheered us very heartily and went off cheering. It was a touching and beautiful sight." Now it seemed that the same troops were destined to return to their barracks in England without ever having to confront the enemy.

A. W. Kinglake, a reporter during the war, describes the irony of the situation that existed in the summer of 1853: "England had become so eager for conflict that the idea of desisting from the war merely because the war had ceased to be necessary was not tolerable to the people."

The Battle of Sinope

The Russian fleet based at Sebastopol helped the allied governments out of their dilemma by providing an excuse to wage war after all. On November 27, 1853, the Russian fleet left its moorings. Under the command of Admiral Paul Nakhimov, the fleet sailed to the Turkish Black Sea port of Sinope. There, on November 30, it found a weak and outdated wooden Turkish fleet lying in the harbor. Nakhimov's five modern battleships proceeded to attack both the town and the Turkish fleet. While the Russian battleships fired upon the town, smaller Russian ships, frigates, and steamers blockaded Sinope Bay in order to prevent any Turkish ships from escaping the destruction raining down upon them from the Russian naval guns.

At the end of the naval action, the Turkish fleet no longer existed. Four thousand Turkish sailors were dead, and the town itself was badly damaged. Only one small Turkish ship escaped the carnage and delivered news of the disaster to the British and the French.

British troops (below, left) receive an enthusiastic farewell from British citizens as they depart for the Crimea. (Below) Russian ships attack the Turkish port of Sinope, annihilating the Turkish fleet and damaging the town.

Allies Furious over "Massacre" at Sinope

The destruction of the Turkish fleet was humiliating for the sultan. It was even more humiliating for the English and the French, whose fleets were supposed to protect the Turkish navy. Now the allied forces could only search for survivors at Sinope and take them to British field hospitals where they were attended to by allied physicians.

A cry of indignation immediately arose from Britain: The "massacre" of Sinope had to be revenged. In London, Lord Clarendon declared: "The feelings of horror which this dreadful carnage could not fail to create, have been general throughout all ranks and classes of Her Majesty's subjects in this country."

Elections were held in Britain, and Lord Aberdeen, the peace-seeking British prime minister who had attempted to prevent Britain from engaging in hostilities, was soon replaced by the more aggressive Lord Palmerston. Palmerston appealed to the nationalist feelings of the English people. He and his cabinet colleagues whipped the British population to war pitch in order to gain support for a war that there was no longer a reason to fight. Finally, late in March 1854, England and France declared war against Russia.

The tsar of Russia, like the leaders of Britain and France, had not expected that Russian demands on Turkey in 1853 would lead to war the following year. Once hostilities were certain, however, Nicholas welcomed war and made every effort to increase popular support for the war. Unlike the English and French leaders, Tsar Nicholas appealed to his people on religious grounds. He announced that "Russia fights not for the things of this world, but for the Faith. England and France have ranged themselves on the side of the enemies of Christianity, against Russia fighting for the orthodox faith."

In the summer of 1854, long after Russian troops had evacuated Turkish territory and the Turkish army had demonstrated its ability to defend itself against the Russians without outside assistance, the armies of England, France, Russia, and Turkey prepared for combat. Before the war ended, hundreds of thousands of troops lost their lives. The reputations of numerous high-ranking officers in each of the armies suffered. Animosities aroused by the war helped to poison the relations of the combatants for the remainder of the nineteenth century. Moreover, the original dispute, the quarrel over control of the holy places in Palestine, was all but forgotten. It disappeared before the flood of horrors brought about by the armies that waged war in the Crimean peninsula.

CHAPTER TWO

Arms and Armies

A
t the beginning of the Crimean conflict, France had an army of approximately 280,000 infantry and 60,000 cavalry. Eventually, about 63,000 of the infantrymen saw service in Turkey and in Russia. The French cavalry did not participate in the Crimean War.

Napoleon III's army was experienced and well trained for battle conditions. Many of his soldiers and officers had seen years of service in Algeria, a colony obtained by France in 1830. As a result of its colonial wars, the French army was alert and well led. The French officers also understood the need to keep the troops well provisioned and well cared for lest their morale and their fighting abilities diminish.

Therefore, as the historian Christopher Hibbert writes, the French army

> landed in the Crimean peninsula with wagons, ambulances, crates of medicines, supplies and comforts; heaps of tents and planks for hutting (wood for constructing temporary buildings) were seen in neat rows along the harbour walls, making an English officer demand in envious exasperation if the French had come to colonize the country.

French weapons were the most modern available. Most French soldiers were equipped with the rifle-barreled Minié gun. The Minié was far more accurate at greater distances than some of the weapons that the British and all the weapons that the Russian soldiers used during the war. This was because the Minié had spiral grooves inside the barrel.

Marshal Saint-Arnaud, leader of the French army, was known for his brutality in battle. Saint-Arnaud led a well-supplied and experienced army into the Crimean War.

Leading the French army was Armand-Jacques Leroy de Saint-Arnaud, marshal of France, a veteran of France's colonial wars. During his early career, his harsh treatment of Algerian prisoners earned Saint-Arnaud a reputation for brutality. His ruthless tactics appealed to Louis Napoleon Bonaparte, who used the marshal's skills to obtain the imperial throne of France in 1852.

Although Saint-Arnaud participated jointly with the British in the Crimean War and many French soldiers were transported on British ships, the French general refused to permit any of his troops to come under British command. In addition he did not share his strategic thinking with his British colleagues. This he shared only with his primary subordinates, General François Canrobert, General Pierre Bosquet, and the cavalry commander, General Morris. All these men were experienced soldiers who had earned their ranks by demonstrating their abilities during active military service. Although the French would play only a minor role during the Battle of Balaclava, the one effort they made on behalf of the British cavalry was of critical importance to the survivors of the Charge of the Light Brigade.

The British Army

In sharp contrast to the French, the British army was a parade-grounds army, ill suited for modern warfare. It had not engaged in combat since the Napoleonic wars at the beginning of the century, and its military thinking had remained unchanged for forty years. Since the British relied mainly on their powerful navy for defense, their army was the smallest of the European powers. The British army consisted of only between thirty and thirty-five thousand men at the beginning of the Crimean campaign and had almost no emergency reserves. Disease, wounds, and deaths soon diminished its size.

The British army that prepared to sail for Turkey in February 1854 was not, in fact, a cohesive military organization. Instead, it consisted of a number of distinct divisions that had not been trained to act together. Furthermore, their training consisted of drills that emphasized parade techniques: marching together in tight formations and wearing gloriously colorful uniforms. These uniforms were designed to impress parade onlookers and enhance the reputations of the officers, especially the cavalry commanders, who selected the dress of their divisions.

Official army regulations supported the British army's emphasis on looks rather than on fighting. For example, the rules regarding appearance applied to tight belts and trousers and the acceptable amount of facial hair. The stocks, or tight leather collars that soldiers were required to wear around their necks, prevented the soldiers from turning their heads so that they would look identical on parade. The stocks also made it difficult for the troops to perform as soldiers, rather than as mannikins, on the field of battle.

In a sarcastic observation, historian C. E. Vulliamy argues that this attention to appearance took precedence over the need to supply the army with tents or medical supplies:

> In the early days of 1854 England was already preparing her armies for the field. Important orders were issued from the Horse Guards [the seat of command in London]: "A clear space of two inches must be left between the corner of the mouth and whiskers, when whiskers are grown. The chin, the underlip, and at least two inches of the upper part of the throat must be clean shaven, so that no hair can be seen above the stock in that place."

The government's attention to the uniform appearance of its troops reflected another attitude toward the individual soldiers. They were regarded as something less than human. Brutal control, exercised through floggings and other physical punishments,

The British army heavily emphasized the importance of its soldiers' appearance while ignoring their effectiveness in battle.

Pomposity of the British Command

The British High Command of the 1850s consisted of a group of aristocrats who almost to a man had never had any military training nor had they led large formations of men into battle. They believed, and so did the British government, that their aristocratic lineage in itself entitled them to command men.

Their families bought them commissions for fabulous sums of money, often when they were little more than boys. They considered their units to be their private showpieces and were always looking for more prestigious units to purchase. Through all these transactions, the aristocrats showed scorn and contempt for the volunteer private soldiers who were the well-disciplined, loyal, and patriotic backbone of the British army but with whom they never mingled.

There were at the time many able British officers. Most of them had been trained and then served in the British army in India. Because of this Eastern experience and because they were not of the aristocratic class, Lord Raglan and his staff regarded the officers of the Army of India as inferiors and did not select them for command positions.

The British army officers treated their troops as they would treat toy soldiers. They should always look as if they were about to parade before an audience: The soldiers wore uncomfortable clothing, leather stocks around their necks to keep their heads high, and tight trousers—even when they were hauling heavy loads or digging trenches.

Lord Lucan at least stayed in the field with his men until he was recalled to London. Lord Cardigan kept his private yacht docked in Balaclava harbor. He slept there every night on clean linen sheets and ate elegant meals prepared for him by his private French chef.

The British officers, led by Lord Raglan, the overall British commander, had no idea whatever of the meaning of military strategy or tactics. What little they knew they had learned during the Napoleonic wars forty years earlier, and they saw no reason to change their beliefs. They went off to war with no maps of the area they planned to attack; no transport for carrying food to the troops in the field; no local money with which to buy supplies; insufficient cavalry for effective deployment; and no plans for dealing with epidemics, winter conditions, or care for the sick and wounded. Nor had they any intentions of cooperating with their French allies with whom they went off to fight.

When the blunders of these officers were exposed and they were criticized for their shortcomings, they were outraged. They were furious that traditional procedures should come under scrutiny, since they had stood the British army in good stead for hundreds of years. Instead of acknowledging their errors and correcting them, they fought back against their attackers on the pages of London newspapers. Meanwhile the real victims of these self-serving and pompous officers, the British soldiers themselves, died by the thousands trying to capture Sebastopol from the Russians.

disciplined the troops. There were virtually no controls to curtail the occasional violent or capricious behavior of ignorant or vicious officers.

The chaotic and brutal treatment of British soldiers was matched by an alarming inefficiency in supplying them with food, clothing, and equipment. Unlike the more organized bureaucracy of the French army, the direction of the army in London was in the hands of a large number of inefficient departments, the directors of which tried to keep tight control over expenditures intended for the troops in the field. Clear-cut systems of supply, transportation, or medical aid did not exist. As a result the British government could not properly feed, clothe, or supply the men and thousands of animals it sent to the Crimea. In general, as Prince Albert, husband of Queen Victoria, complained: "The complications, the muddle, the duplications, the mutual jealousies, and labyrinthine process of supply and control were astonishing."

In addition to these difficulties, the British had only a very limited military medical corps, although most of the doctors who served with the troops did so valiantly and under appalling conditions. Furthermore, unlike the Russian and French armies, English doctors initially had no female nurses to assist them. In England at that time female nurses were regarded as little better than prostitutes. It was unthinkable that they be permitted to serve with the army when the troops left for the Crimea. Florence Nightingale's heroic efforts at the army hospitals at Scutari, and later in the Crimean peninsula itself, began the long process of changing the public conception of the role of nurses and the importance of using proper medical and sanitary procedures to care for the ill British soldier. The primitive conditions and ideas that existed in the British medical corps led to many more men's dying of disease than from wounds. In general, confusion marked the entire administration of the British army in both its medical and its fighting capacities.

Still worse, the British officers were woefully incapable of fulfilling their responsibilities. Rank was determined by the price an officer could pay for it, not by his success in battle. Wealthy families simply bought commissions in the army for their sons so that the young men could enter one of the few socially acceptable professions for upper-class men. For example,

British nurse Florence Nightingale worked tenaciously to care for soldiers. Her valiant efforts helped to improve both the public's attitude toward female nurses and the inferior state of the British medical corps.

The Purchase System

The ability of the British to purchase military commissions resulted in officers who were unprepared to lead men into battle. Because their purchases were regarded as private property, it was virtually impossible to remove them from command, even if they proved incompetent or committed serious crimes. Lord Brudenell, later Lord Cardigan, found himself in trouble with the law during the 1830s. However, when the powerful duke of Wellington intervened on Lord Cardigan's behalf, he was restored to his place in the regiment. The *Times* of London was horrified by the proceedings and by the restoration of this incompetent officer to his regiment. This quotation is from Cecil Woodham-Smith's *The Reason Why:*

How came Lord Brudenell—an officer of no pretensions or experience comparable to those of a hundred other gentlemen who had seen and beaten a foreign enemy—how came such an unripe gallant as this to be put over the heads of so many worthier candidates, to be forced into a command for which, we may now say, he has proved himself utterly incompetent. This officer was a man of no experience. We are told he never did regimental duty for more than three years of his life. He was not less incapacitated for command by temper, than by ignorance of his duty as a commanding officer, both professional and moral. Such a man ought never to be placed at the head of a regiment.

Lord Cardigan's father paid forty thousand pounds, today the equivalent of over $500,000, for his son's first military appointment. Thus, the very system by which they obtained their ranks condemned them to ineffectiveness.

Once commissioned, these men regarded their association with their divisions as an obligation of their class and rarely served more than a few months at a time with their troops. These officers preferred to spend their time on their own estates in England and among their upper-class peers.

Consequently, most of the general officers in charge of the British army had neither seen field action nor led men in battle. They were old. They had poor vision, lacked military understanding, and stubbornly refused to request the assistance of younger men of the middle class who had served as professional soldiers in the Army of India.

The British general officers who served in the Crimean War generally scorned the study of military history, planning, and strategy. They believed that such detailed study smacked of professionalism; that is, they believed that tradespeople, such as printers and factory owners, had to learn their profession. For the aristocracy, however, characteristics such as bravery and chivalry were acquired by birth through blood and passed by one generation to another. These qualities were the only requirement for a nobleman to lead other men. For them tradition was everything.

This attitude made for curious misunderstandings, since for many officers that tradition included the memory that for centuries France had been Britain's enemy and Russia had been the ally. Many of these old men found it hard to remember that times had changed. As historian Peter Gibbs observes:

> The situation would have been an ideal subject for a farcical play if it were not so tragic. Thus, for example, while the British soldiers received no formal training for the practical realities of war, they did experience some target practice. But, the target was usually a crudely shaped representation of an oversize French grenadier, and the officers would invite their men to stand, never more than a hundred yards away, and try to hit it with a ball shot from their muskets.

British officers found it difficult to ask the French for assistance at moments of military crisis because the French had been the enemy for so many centuries. They never accepted the French as true allies, only as necessary collaborators during the Crimean War.

Lord Raglan

Lord Raglan, born Fitzroy Somerset, youngest son of the duke of Beaufort, commander of the British army in the Crimea, was a kindly man of sixty-five who had been an aide to the duke of Wellington forty years earlier. He had lost his right arm during the Battle of Waterloo. Raglan had observed battlefield carnage firsthand, but he had never commanded men in battle.

In 1854 Lord Raglan was the most senior British officer, so the government selected him to lead the British army to the Crimea. Unfortunately, he had spent his last thirty-five years in the army behind a desk at the Horse Guards in the heart of London, seat of command of the British army. At Whitehall Lord Raglan learned nothing about tactics, strategy, military organization, ordnance, or geography. He

Lord Raglan was asked to command the British army in the Crimea, despite his inexperience and lack of basic military skills.

did not even possess a map of the Crimean peninsula when he landed with his troops, and he regarded the use of spies to obtain information as behavior unbefitting a gentleman.

Unlike many of his counterparts, Lord Raglan was aware of his own shortcomings as a military leader. Furthermore, unlike many of his colleagues, he harbored some warm regard for the troops who had fought so well in earlier years. Although he was unable to alter the primitive administrative system that condemned the soldiers to untold suffering, he believed that if he refused to go to the Crimea, someone even less qualified than he would be given command of the British army.

Raglan led a force of five infantry divisions. The five divisional commanders—Sir Richard English; Sir George Cathcart; De Lacy Evans; the duke of Cambridge, a first cousin of Queen Victoria; and George Brown—shared all of Lord Raglan's shortcomings as a soldier and little of his concern for the British army in its entirety.

The British Cavalry

Lord Raglan also commanded a cavalry force made up of a cavalry division that contained a Light and a Heavy Brigade. The horses of the Light Brigade were smaller in stature and weight than those of the Heavy Brigade, and while the Light Brigade generally carried lances, the Heavy Brigade was armed with swords and carbines. The army used the Light Brigade mostly for scouting purposes, while the massive weight and strength of the horses of the Heavy Brigade made them ideal for shock combat, or aiming strong opposition against a particular point in the enemy's position. The Heavy Brigade would be used this way against opposing enemy cavalrymen. Together the two brigades numbered approximately twelve hundred men. Two of the cavalry leaders, Lord Lucan and Lord Cardigan, were destined to play major roles during the Battle of Balaclava.

Lord Lucan and Lord Cardigan were aristocrats who never questioned their own innate ability to lead men, but neither of them had much experience on the battlefield. They expected their regiments to perform according to the rules of the drill book, that is, as if they were on the parade ground. Lord Lucan, in particular, had not even acquainted himself with the proper commands by which to lead his men. However, Lucan and Cardigan had spent a good deal of money to outfit their troops in gorgeous uniforms.

In addition to their lack of military experience, both men were poorly educated; exceptionally stubborn, argumentative, and stupid; and both found it difficult to accept orders. Lucan was described as "conscientious, prejudiced, vindictive, brave, narrow-minded and violent." He was known to his soldiers as

British Dislike of Their Cavalry Officers

John Selby in his book *The Thin Red Line of Balaclava* quotes Captain Lewis Edward Nolan, a popular British cavalry officer, openly criticizing Lord Lucan and Lord Cardigan.

> We all agree that two greater muffs than Lucan and Cardigan could not be; we call Lucan the cautious ass and Cardigan the dangerous ass; Lord Cardigan has as much brains as his boot and is only to equal in want of intellect by his relative the Earl of Lucan; without mincing matters, two such fools to take command could hardly be picked out of the British army; but then, they are Earls!

Historian and journalist A. W. Kinglake describes how he knew and detested Lord Cardigan and Lord Lucan. In his book *The Invasion of the Crimea: Its Origins and an Account of Its Progress Down to the Death of Lord Raglan*, Kinglake provides a clear statement of his low regard for the two earls. Of Cardigan he wrote:

> Among his good qualities was a love of order; but this with him was in such morbid excess, that it constituted a really dangerous foible, involved him from time to time in mischief. He slept on his yacht with a French cook on board. When not only all the officers and men under him but also his divisional chief, were cheerfully bearing the hardships and privations of camp life . . . there surely was cruelty in the idea of placing human beings under the military control of an officer at once so arbitrary and so narrow, but the notion of such a man having been able to purchase for himself a right to hold Englishmen in military subjection, is to my mind, revolting. Lord Cardigan incurred a series of decrees, and was removed from the command of his regiment; but afterwards by the special desire of the Duke of Wellington he was restored to active service.

Kinglake detested Lord Lucan as much as he detested Lord Cardigan. Of Lord Lucan he wrote:

> Lord Lucan was the brother-in-law of Lord Cardigan; but so little beloved by him that in the eyes of cynical London, an arrangement for coupling the one man to the other seemed almost a fell stroke of humour. It might have been thought that, in a free country, the notion of carrying official perverseness to any such extreme length as this must have been nipped in the bud. It was not so. If England was free, she was also very patient of evil institutions, as well as of official misfeasance. She trusted too much to the fitful anger of Parliament, and the chances of remonstrance in print.

"the cautious ass" because of his unwillingness to commit his troops to battle. Lord Cardigan was referred to as "the dangerous ass" because of his willingness to commit his cavalrymen to action under any circumstances. The principal reporter for the *Times* of London in the Crimea, William Howard Russell, called Cardigan "proud, narrow, jealous and self-willed."

As early as 1834 Lord Cardigan had been chastised by the House of Lords for ordering the vicious whipping of a junior officer as punishment for a minor offense. When, through the interference of the duke of Wellington, he was permitted to rejoin his regiment, the *Times* expressed its horror at the reappointment:

> He was not less incapacitated for command by temper, than by ignorance of his duty as a commanding officer, both professional and moral. Such a man ought never to be placed at the head of a regiment.

But Lord Cardigan learned nothing from this momentary setback. During the Crimean War he continued to display the same tragic disregard for the lives of his men.

What made matters even worse was that Lord Lucan and Lord Cardigan were brothers-in-law who detested each other. They made no secret of their mutual hatred. The officers permitted this personal hatred to interfere with their handling of the troops under their commands, often quarreling loudly with one another within the hearing of the two brigades. In fact, according to historian Alexis S. Troubetzkoy:

> Tales emanating from the savage and protracted feud of Lord Cardigan and his brother-in-law, the Earl of Lucan, are legion. Early in the campaign the commander of the Light Brigade and his immediate superior, the commander of the Cavalry Division, ceased speaking to one another. No one could bring reconciliation between the two men, each as proud as Lucifer.

British cavalry leader Lord Cardigan's disregard for the lives of his soldiers and foolhardy tactics earned him the nickname "the dangerous ass."

The deficiencies of the cavalry leaders were well understood by those unfortunate enough to serve under them. Major John Forrest of the Forty-third Dragoon Guards wrote a letter to his family in England on August 27, 1854, describing his feelings toward Lord Lucan:

> We have not much confidence in our Cavalry General and only hope he will allow the Brigadiers to move their own Brigades. . . . Lord Lucan is no doubt a clever, sharp fellow, but he has been so long on the shelf that he has no idea of moving cavalry, does not even know the words of command, and is very self-willed about it, thinks himself right.

The astonishing skill, bravery, loyalty, obedience, and gallantry of the junior officers and the British troopers facilitated the successes that Cardigan's and Lucan's units achieved. These officers and soldiers were men who had selected to serve in the British army as their chosen profession. As a group they were patriotic, loyal, and dedicated to their regiments and their regimental traditions.

The Russian Army in the Crimea

As impossible as it may seem, the many shortcomings of the British army were less serious than those of the Russian army, which was even less capable. Despite its huge size and a general belief in its invincibility, the Russian army of the mid–nineteenth century was ineffective. It was composed of many national groups, and it had no sense of unity. It was weak, inefficient, and poorly led. The officers treated the men brutally, and even during peacetime the death rate was very high. In addition, because Russia had almost no railroad system, the soldiers often were forced to march for many hundreds of miles under terrible conditions to reach their destination.

The Russian army was immense: 678,000 men were under arms, along with 86 squadrons of cavalry and a reserve of 182 battalions. Including additional irregular troops and various auxiliary units, the Russian army consisted of a total of 1,290,000 men.

Unlike most of their British counterparts, Russian common soldiers were drafted into service. They were rough, raw men, mostly serfs, that is, unfree peasants. The tsar's recruiters would comb through a district looking for young men. Often owners of serfs turned over men who were troublemakers. Prisons frequently were emptied to fill the local quota of recruits. Most Russian families regarded recruitment into the army as a lifelong jail sentence. The term of service was twenty-five years, conditions were brutal, and most soldiers never saw their families again.

This long term of service meant that those who survived grew old in the army. Many of the soldiers serving in the tsar's armies during the Crimean War were too old for the long, forced marches to the Crimean peninsula or for the rigors of the campaign that followed.

Like the British army, the Russian army was steeped in the traditions of the Napoleonic period. Blind obedience to orders, fighting in tight formations, and ignoring the agony of fallen comrades during combat characterized both these armies. In the 1790s the great Russian general Aleksandr Vasilyevich Suvorov fought valiantly and successfully against the French military conquerors of Italy. Suvorov taught his men to "despise the bullet in favour of the bayonet" and his officers to rely on "intuition, rapidity and impact." The Russian army followed these maxims in the 1850s and died in alarming numbers. According to one Russian officer, "while the soldier in the West [this was increasingly true for the British army in India and in the French army] was taught to develop his presence of mind and individuality, the quality the Russians valued above all things was to be trained to act in masses."

Russian soldiers generally went into battle in tightly formed columns, with their bayonets at the ready. Often they were drunk as they prepared to charge because the officers passed out alcohol

Russian Military Training

Western leaders considered the Russian army to be an extraordinarily strong war machine. Each year the Russian government drafted eighty thousand recruits who then served for a period of twenty-five years. The army certainly appeared formidable when it marched on the parade ground in formation in order to please the tsar during inspections.

The size of the army, however, obscured its many defects. The soldiers received little effective training. Their weapons were of extremely poor quality. Since only two rifle factories existed in all of Russia, many soldiers did not even receive old-style weapons with which to defend themselves. The Russian soldiers were expected to make their own shirts, boots, and underwear from materials supplied to them by the army. New materials were seldom issued, and their uniforms often were ragged. In addition, their food was dull and of poor quality and illness was frequent.

Despite these terrible conditions, however, the Russian army was obedient. The great mass of the Russian army was kept in line by frequent floggings and other forms of corporal punishment, which the West was beginning to look on with disfavor.

The army was forced to march over enormous distances, since railroads barely existed in Russia. Every year thousands of recruits died from exhaustion, starvation, and exposure. The troops generally were sent into battle fortified by double rations of strong alcohol to increase their bravery in the face of the enemy.

Russian officers and their troops were not trained to adapt to changing military situations and strategies. During the Crimean War, they, like the British, continued to use military techniques of the Napoleonic period. Great numbers of Russian soldiers were slaughtered because their largely untrained, illiterate officers did not know how to use their great armies effectively.

before the battle. The alcohol was intended to dull the horror of viewing hundreds of their comrades falling around them. (Alcohol also was routinely issued to British and French troops, but it was neither distributed nor consumed in the quantities ascribed to their Russian counterparts.) Huge numbers of Russian troops died in combat compared to their counterparts in the British and French armies. In part this was because the Russians were armed with the old, smooth-bore, barrel-loading musket, which was ineffective except at very short distances. On many occasions the Russian troops were cut down by enemy infantry fire before they could come within musket range.

Mistreatment of Russian Soldiers

The almost unlimited human resources in Russia encouraged other abuses of the soldiers. The historian Constantin de Grunwald observes:

There is not an army in Europe where the death rate is as high as in the Russian army . . . even during a period of peace . . . the long marches, the harsh punishments, the cold, which caused great suffering to the soldiers because of their shaven heads, (to keep them free of lice and other pests) their lack of resilience to disease and low morale.

All of these factors contributed to the relative inefficiency of the various units of the Russian army during the Crimean War.

The overall leadership of the Russian army was in the hands of General Prince Alexander Menshikov, a favorite of Tsar Nicholas I. Menshikov was sixty-five years old. He had risen to high office through his friendship and devotion to the tsar's family, whom he had served as early as the Napoleonic wars. Menshikov had also previously been an admiral and an ambassador. He had retired from active military service thirty years before he was selected to lead the Russian army in the Crimea in 1854.

An "Arrogant and Autocratic" Leader

He was entirely ill suited to head the Russian military. He was poorly educated and possessed no military skills. According to the historian Christopher Hibbert, Menshikov was "arrogant and autocratic and he was not popular with his men; and his officers had long since learned not to offer him any advice." In addition, because he had been castrated by a Turkish bullet during an earlier campaign, he hated the Turks with such intensity that it was difficult for him to assess how best to fight them. In the earlier stages of the war, before the arrival of British and French troops, huge Russian armies under his direction had sustained defeats at the hands of the Turks.

Menshikov, like his counterpart Raglan in the British army, also had a cavalry force under his command in the Crimea. Like Raglan he demonstrated no particular skill in handling the cavalry. The Russian cavalry was entrusted to General Pavel Liprandi who, like Lords Lucan and Cardigan, also was a master of parade group techniques. Liprandi, Ryzhov, and the many other Russian officers under Menshikov's command were trained never to question orders and never to show initiative.

The weakness of the Russian army was Britain's greatest asset during the Battle of Balaclava. As historian Albert Seaton observes of that army:

The story is one of incompetence and cowardice on the part of the Russian high command. There was a total lack of determined leadership and professional ability. Many of the Russian generals were brave men and numbers of them were shot down leading their columns. But regimental officers, rank and file were ill-trained, ill-equipped and fought with their customary doggedness.

Additional Weaknesses in the Russian Army

At the onset of the Crimean War, Britain and France considered the very size of the Russian army a danger to their own interests. Neither had an understanding of the weaknesses of the giant military. The following quote, taken from Albert Seaton's book *The Crimean War, a Russian Chronicle*, graphically reveals the weaknesses of the tsar's forces.

> The small staff organization in the capital, known as His Majesty's Suite for Quartermaster Affairs, was the only permanent general staff body in existence but its responsibilities covered the movement and quartering of troops, reconnaissance, intelligence and finance. The Russian Army's main training ground was the drill square; even its battle tactics were performed as parade evolutions. Most officers appear to have been without higher education or intellectual development. Little was demanded of them beyond obedience, and performing routine duties according to the regulations; youthful enthusiasm was soon dulled by boredom and drink; they were products of a system which regarded any tendency toward independent thought as heresy.

Alexis S. Troubetzkoy's book *The Road to Balaklava* describes the Russian army recruitment system. The details help to explain the army's poor performance during the battle.

> The Russian army was not the world's best war machine at the time. It was ponderous and clumsy; it was permeated with corruption, deficiencies and inefficiencies. The mass of enlisted men were conscripted from the ranks of factory labourers, peasants and privately-owned serfs. In the decades preceding the Crimean War, an average of eighty thousand draftees were inducted annually to serve for twenty five years. Landowners often sent off rebellious serfs; communes arranged for the induction of troublesome peasants; courts used the army as a prison without bars for religious offenders. Thus, with reason, the Russian people looked on induction into the army as almost equivalent to penal servitude for life and bewailed [believed that they would die during their service in the army] as dead their sons whom the army took. Often they never saw them again.

Turkish Army

The final participant in the Battle of Balaclava was the Turkish army, which played a critical role during the opening moments of the attack. Much like the Russian army, the Turkish army was a mixture of the many national groups that made up the Turkish Empire: soldiers from Egypt, Algeria, the Asiatic portions of the empire, as well as Turks from Anatolia. Some were well trained. Most were poorly trained draftees who had been ripped away from their family farms and intended by the sultan to provide cannon fodder for the government.

The Turkish officer corps was not significantly better trained for warfare than were the recruits. Historian Peter Gibbs writes that as the Russians began their invasion of Turkey in 1853, the Turkish officer corps was largely absent:

> A lieutenant-general, two major generals and a colonel were struggling with the alphabet in one of the military schools in Constantinople. Admittedly they were still mere youths,—all under twenty-one but they were fortunate enough to have fathers who were ministers of the state.

On the whole, the Turkish army was poorly fed, poorly armed, and indifferently led by officers with only slightly less training than their Russian or British counterparts. The sultan was, however, fortunate in having Omar Pasha as his main general.

Russian officers draft soldiers for the Crimean War. Conscription was often used as punishment, and the unwilling enlisted men contributed to the ineptitude of the Russian army.

Omar Pasha

Omar Pasha had been born Michael Lattas in Austria in 1806. Lattas served in the Austrian army, became a tutor for children of wealthy Turks, became a Muslim, and along the way demonstrated amazing military abilities.

Omar Pasha, commander of the Turkish army, was a skilled military leader whose capabilities earned him a royal title and the trust of the sultan.

In 1834 Lattas took the name of Omar. He rose quickly within the Turkish army, and by the time of the Crimean War, he was a generalissimo, or overall commander of the sultan's armies, and had been given the title of highness, which gave him the status of royalty in the sultan's court. The sultan placed extraordinary faith in his general and his troops. They, in turn, displayed remarkable fortitude in driving the Russians from the Turkish provinces in the early months of the war.

They did so well that Lord Raglan entrusted Turkish troops with the critical task of manning the most remote, exposed defenses at Balaclava. Brave under fire, the badly treated Turkish troops nevertheless provided meritorious service to Britain.

These then were the armies that prepared to engage in warfare. As the military leaders gathered together their men, food, and transportation, the civilian leaders tried to decide where the troops would clash and what their war aims actually were.

CHAPTER THREE

The Setting

Men thought that what was wanting in bayonets might possibly be eked out with the spade.

A. W. Kinglake, *The Invasion of the Crimea*

War was declared against Russia on March 23, 1854. Patriotism was stirred. But what was the objective of the war? Where would the war be fought? Finally, three months after the actual declaration of war against Russia was issued, the British objective of the war was mentioned unofficially in the House of Lords. In June, Lord Lyndhurst told his colleagues that "in no event, except that of extreme necessity, ought we to make peace without previously destroying the Russian fleet in the Black Sea and laying prostrate the fortifications by which it is defended."

Because the statement did not come from the prime minister, there was some confusion about whether this was official policy, but the *Times* of London published Lyndhurst's statement as the official British position on July 23, 1854. On that day the newspaper stated that "the broad policy of the war consists in striking at the very heart of the Russian power in the East, and that heart is Sebastopol."

Soon afterwards the British government itself issued an official announcement that identified the destruction of Sebastopol as the objective of the war with Russia. France immediately endorsed that position. The new French emperor, Napoleon III, hoped to gain both British friendship and military glory by sending his troops to the Crimean peninsula.

Both governments believed that the destruction of Sebastopol would revenge the terrible disaster to the Turkish fleet at Sinope and their own failure to protect the Turkish fleet, and prevent

Russia from threatening British interests in the Mediterranean. France and Britain also hoped that a Russian defeat would put an end to Russian dreams of expansion for the foreseeable future.

Allied Armies Land in the Crimea

On September 14, 1854, six months after the formal declaration of war against Russia and almost a year after the Battle of Sinope, allied armies, more than sixty thousand strong, landed on the Crimean coast. The troopships anchored in Calamita Bay, about forty-five miles north of Sebastopol, and the soldiers began to disembark. Although General Menshikov had been warned that the allied armies intended to invade, he sent a letter to the tsar, anxiously waiting in St. Petersburg for news of the war, that in his view, it was too late in the campaigning season for the British and the French to land. As a result of Russian incompetence, the allied armies landed unmolested and prepared to march south toward Sebastopol.

General Menshikov soon realized the error of his assumptions and determined to destroy the allied army. Consequently, he drew up a large Russian force of about thirty-eight thousand, complete with many cannons and several cavalry divisions on the south bank of the Alma River, one of a series of shallow rivers that the British, French, and Turks would have to cross before reaching Sebastopol. On September 20 the two armies found each other on opposite sides of the river.

The two armies sat facing each other for many hours in the hot sun, neither side willing to begin the attack. Finally, about one o'clock in the afternoon the battle began. Soon a small party of French, under General Bosquet on the extreme right of the allied line and closest to the water's edge, crossed the river and managed to scale what the Russians believed to be an insurmountable cliff.

They worked their way up a winding path on the face of the cliff and reached a plateau about 350 feet above sea level. Once there, these veterans of many colonial campaigns were in a position to attack the weak left flank of Menshikov's army and force it to retreat.

When news of the French fording of the river arrived, General Menshikov rode off in a fury to defend the end of his line, four miles distant. The British took advantage of the moment and began to ford the river facing a place called the Great Redoubt, a detached fieldwork located on an especially high point above the Alma River where the Russians had placed their cannons.

Although they suffered many casualties from the Russian musket fire raining down on them, the British succeeded in crossing the river, climbing the southern embankment, and capturing the redoubt, or primitive fortification. The Russians fled

the field of battle in confusion. The Battle of the Alma thus became the first allied victory of the Crimean War.

At this point the allied leaders began to quarrel. General Raglan wanted to press the allied advantage achieved at the Alma. The British general wanted to attack Sebastopol immediately while it lay undefended, abandoned by the Russian army retreating to the interior of the Crimean peninsula. However, the mortally ill French general Saint-Arnaud refused. He insisted instead that the allies march around Sebastopol and attack the fortress from the south, which he assumed was less well defended than the northern side of the fortress.

Raglan reluctantly agreed to Saint-Arnaud's plan. The march around Sebastopol ultimately brought the British army to the small, picturesque port of Balaclava. Balaclava is situated on the southern Black Sea coast of the Crimean peninsula. It is about six miles southeast from the port and base of Sebastopol.

Lord Raglan decided that the tiny port would serve the immediate supply needs of his army. This assumption was based on the fact that the port was very deep and could accommodate even the *Agamemnon*, the largest of the British ships with the fleet. In addition, because the British assumed that Sebastopol would fall almost immediately, the British army did not think it

Shortly after landing on the coast of the Crimea, British and French troops defeat the Russians during the Battle of the Alma.

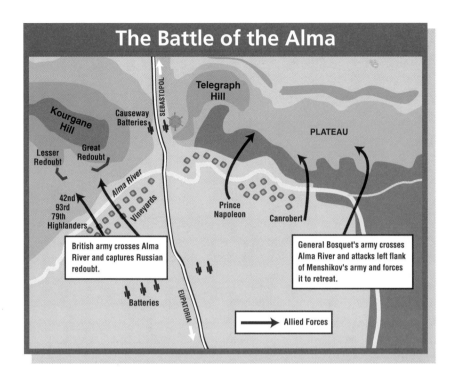

The Battle of the Alma

British army crosses Alma River and captures Russian redoubt.

General Bosquet's army crosses Alma River and attacks left flank of Menshikov's army and forces it to retreat.

→ Allied Forces

needed a large, well-equipped naval facility to provision the troops. The plan was that all supplies delivered from England would reach the British army through the port of Balaclava.

Allies Begin Siege of Sebastopol

From the start, the allied attack on Sebastopol was handled poorly. Since General Menshikov and his soldiers had deserted Sebastopol, only a handful of soldiers and sailors, reinforced by civilian men, women, and children, defended it. An immediate attack would have been successful.

Rather than attack, the allies decided to besiege the weak southern fortifications of the naval base. Laboriously the soldiers and sailors unloaded the siege materials from the ships. Slowly they hauled them up to the heights overlooking Sebastopol. As a result, the allies did not begin to bombard Sebastopol until October 17, almost a month after their victory at the Alma. By that time the Russian army had recovered psychologically from its defeat and had returned to reinforce the Sebastopol garrison. By then, also, General Todleben, an expert in siege warfare, had erected massive defenses around the land side of the southern half of the Russian port, which now made it extremely difficult for the allied armies to storm.

The deadly allied bombardment began on October 17 and continued for three days; guns fired at Sebastopol both from the allied positions from the heights above the port and from the English ships at sea. By October 20, however, it was clear that the mission had failed. After each bombardment to soften up the Russian defenses, the defenders, including the civilian population, worked heroically in the dark of night to repair the breaches in the fortifications.

British hopes for an early victory faded. General Raglan and his staff began to realize that the war would drag on for many more months. With some anxiety they also realized that the tiny port of Balaclava would need to be protected to allow the allied armies to be resupplied.

The Russian armies, on the other hand, were heartened by their ability to withstand the terrible three-day bombardment. They sensed that they had an opportunity to drive the British out of the Crimea by attacking them at their weakest point, their supply base at Balaclava.

Russian generals under Menshikov massed their infantry and cavalry units in order to carry out their attack. Menshikov believed that the sheer number of Russians would destroy the British army already reduced through battle and disease. Lord

The allied armies' fleet crowds the port of Balaclava. The allies mistakenly expected the attack on Sebastopol to be an easy victory and thought the tiny port would suffice.

An Engineer Provides the Defenses for Sebastopol

The Russian fortification at Sebastopol, developed by an engineering officer and built by troops as well as civilians, endured a three-day attack by the allies.

The defense of Sebastopol rested on the able shoulders of a Russian engineering officer, Franz Eduard Ivanovitch Todleben. He has been described as a military genius. Within a few short weeks following the defeat of the Russian army at the Alma River, he galvanized the spirits of the civilians as well as the military forces in Sebastopol to build defensive works able to withstand the terrible bombardment of October 17–20, 1854. The historian C. E. Vulliamy provides an excellent portrait of Todleben in his book *Crimea*.

Todleben is a man with a very military aspect, an open, sensitive countenance, plain though courteous manners, a merry disposition, a rapid eye, cool judgment in the face of danger, a marked aversion to plotters and rogues and a noble severity adequately restrained by humane principles. His genius and originality consisted in a totally fresh view of the nature of defense. He may justly be called the originator of the idea that a fortress is to be considered, not as a walled town but as an entrenched position, intimately connected with the offensive and defensive capacities of an army and as susceptible of alteration as the formation of troops in battle or manoeuvre.

Raglan assumed that the defenses he had prepared around Balaclava were sufficient to withstand a Russian attack. Both leaders were wrong. The battle about to take place demonstrated to the world that military training, experience, and knowledge were far more important in modern warfare than high birth and wealth.

The Balaclava Plain

The Battle of Balaclava took place largely on the Balaclava Plain. The plain lies about six miles to the south of the naval base of Sebastopol and about a mile and a quarter from the port of Balaclava itself. The area between the two ports is quite mountainous. Many rivers run through the region and many gaps in the mountains open onto the Balaclava Plain from the north.

William Howard Russell, the chief *Times* reporter covering the British army, sent a letter to his editor on October 15, 1854, in which he describes the ominous nature of the hills and mountains overlooking Balaclava:

> At three or four miles' distance from Balaclava, the valley is swallowed up in a mountain gorge and deep ravines, above which rise tiers after tiers of desolate white rock, garnished now and then by bits of scanty herbage, and spreading away toward the east and south, where they attain Alpine dimensions.

The newspaperman immediately recognized the potential danger that the mountains represented to the small British force at Balaclava:

> It is very easy for an army at the Belbek [River] or in command of the road to Mackenzie's farm to debouch through these gorges at any time upon the plain from the neck of the valley or to march from Sebastopol by the Tchernaya [River], and to advance along it toward Balaclava where they would meet the Turkish redoubts on the south and to the left the Fedioukine Hills upon which further enemy emplacements could be established.

While Russell described the dangerous situation to his editor in London, Lord Raglan took steps to defend his exposed rear position. He posted small groups of men in strategically critical positions around the approaches to the port of Balaclava. The vast majority of his forces, of course, remained on the heights above the plain, maintaining the siege of Sebastopol.

The first group of defenders guarded the immediate approach to Balaclava. A steep, dirt road, a little over a mile long, led from Balaclava up to the little village of Kadikoi at the entrance to the gorge above the harbor. Raglan ordered the Highland Scots, perhaps 450 in all, along with some Turkish troops, to be placed here.

A battery of guns called the marine artillery defended both the infantry units and the road that led to the port. Lord Raglan

A Journalist Describes the Battlefield

In one of his letters to the *Times*, William Howard Russell describes with great clarity the view of the battle seen from the crest of the Sapoune Heights. The extract is from a letter dated October 25, 1854, which Russell wrote on the evening following the battle. This report describes the scene to anxious families in England.

Supposing the spectator, then, [were] to take his stand on one of the heights . . . he would see the town of Balaklava, with its scanty shipping, its narrow strip of water, and its old forts on his right hand; immediately below he would behold the valley and plain of coarse meadow land, occupied by our cavalry tents, and stretching from the base of the ridge on which he stood to the foot of the formidable heights at the other side; he would see the French trenches lined with Zouaves a few feet beneath, and distant from him, on the slope of the hill; a Turkish redoubt lower down, then another in the valley, then, in a line with it, some angular earthworks, then, in succession, the other two redoubts up to Canrobert's Hill. At the distance of two or two and a half miles across the valley there is an abrupt rocky mountain range of most irregular and picturesque formations, covered with scanty brushwood here and there, or rising into barren pinnacles and plateaux of rock. A patch of blue sea is caught in between the overhanging cliffs of Balaklava as they close in the entrance to the harbour on the right. The camp of the Marines, pitched on the hill side more than 1000 feet above the level of the sea, is opposite to you, as your back is turned to Sebastopol and your right side toward Balaklava. On the road leading up the valley, close to the entrance of the town, and beneath these hills, is the encampment of the 93rd Highlanders.

placed these guns on a range of hills about a thousand feet above the valley. The battery, a group of four to eight guns, was not far from and overlooked both the village and the road to the port, a road that had been built along the base of the range of hills on which the battery rested.

To the north of Kadikoi and running in a southeasterly direction rose a high ground called the Causeway Heights. The heights rose about three hundred feet above the Balaclava Plain and separated the plain into what were known as the North Valley and the South Valley.

The Causeway Heights were of great strategic importance to the protection of Balaclava. The high ground ran the length of the plain, then eastward, across the Tchernaya River, and past several ranges of hills and mountain passes through which the Russians could begin an attack. To the west, the road dipped to the floor of the North Valley and then ran up the Sapoune Ridge and on to Sebastopol.

The Woronzov Road was the best surfaced route in the Crimea. It linked Sebastopol with the towns of Baidar and Yalta. The road ran along the crest of the causeway and it was an essential means of transporting military supplies to the area around Sebastopol. In a countryside otherwise connected largely by unpaved paths, the Woronzov was the only modern roadway. The British knew that the Russians were beginning to place field guns in various spots in the hills above the Woronzov Road. Raglan also knew that if the Russians gained control of the road, they could easily gain control of the small village of Kamara.

Kamara lay at the end of the South Valley about two miles from Kadikoi where the Highland Regiment defended the entrance to the port. If taken over by the Russians, Kamara could serve as an enemy base from which to launch an attack on Balaclava. The heights, according to Christopher Hibbert,

were not only vital to the defence of Balaclava and the rear and flank of the army's position but also to its line of communication. For to lose the Heights would mean to loose the one good road across the plain leading to the camps and siege works overlooking Sebastopol.

Russian soldiers spend a quiet night in their camp at Sebastopol, site of the heavy but unsuccessful bombardment by allied forces.

Construction of a Series of Redoubts

British engineers began construction of a series of redoubts, temporary military emplacements for relatively small groups of men, built hastily with whatever construction materials were at hand. These primitive fortifications were often protected by little more than mounds of earth from the surrounding area. The first of these was called Canrobert's Hill, named after the general who took over French forces when General Saint-Arnaud died. Canrobert's Hill was the largest of the redoubts. It also was the most remote from the port and therefore the one most likely to be attacked first by the Russians. When it was completed, Canrobert's Hill was large enough to hold six hundred Turkish troops led by several British artillerymen, three 12-pound field guns, and supplies.

The redoubt was on a rise of ground about five hundred feet above sea level. From this elevation the Turkish soldiers who defended it could observe an enemy force making its way around the Causeway Heights and also any movements of Russian troops near the village of Kamara.

Alexander William Kinglake was another of the reporters sent by the *Times* of London to observe the war. Years later, at the request of the widow of Lord Raglan, Kinglake wrote a major history of its events. Kinglake examined the earthen works on Canrobert's Hill and took exception to their location. He believed that the engineers placed the first redoubt so as to be "perilously exposed to any artillery which might be placed in a battery on the neighboring ridge of Kamara." It also was far enough away from the British base at the foot of the Sapoune Heights to make the sending of reinforcements very difficult under a combat situation.

The other five redoubts were known simply by their numbers, two through six. About three hundred Turkish soldiers defended redoubts two, three, and four. They also had several heavy naval guns for protection. British artillerymen commanded both the weapons and the Turkish soldiers. At the time of the Battle of Balaclava, redoubts five and six had not been completed and were not defended or attacked.

The six redoubts lay in a small chain along the heights that separated the North and South Valleys and spanned a distance of about two miles. Kinglake also criticized this arrangement. The farthest of them, he writes, "offered the enemy a license of some hours' duration for any enterprise in the plain of Balaclava upon which he might think fit to venture." In addition, the redoubts were too far from one another to offer mutual support in case of attack.

Despite the strategic importance of the redoubts to the British, Lord Raglan did not ensure that his engineers design them in an effective manner. They were hastily constructed and poorly fortified. In fact redoubt number two was built in less than a day. The engineers did not oversee the removal of the brush that surrounded the redoubts. Therefore, enemy forces could approach fairly closely without alerting the defenders to their presence.

It was something of a surprise that Lord Raglan entrusted the defense of these important redoubts to Turkish troops. Like most English soldiers, he did not hold the Turkish army in high regard. In fact, according to historian Cecil Woodham-Smith:

> His contempt and dislike for them were intense. . . . To Lord Raglan Turks were bandits, and officers of the Bengal and Bombay Armies only one degree more acceptable. The Turkish troops had been treated with contempt, their commissariat arrangements were almost non-existent, they were half-starved, and their morale was low.

Yet, under the direction of Omar Pasha, the Turkish army had displayed remarkable military prowess against the Russians during the siege of Silistria. Various officers told Lord Raglan that Turkish troops did well when they had walled areas to defend. In fact, General Cannon, who served with the Turks in 1853, assured Raglan that "though they were not always reliable in the open they could be trusted behind a defensive work." Against his better judgment, then, and because he did not want to remove British troops from siege operations, Raglan decided to assign the task of guarding the redoubts to the Turks.

The last of the redoubts, unfinished number six, lay not far from a rise of land called the Sapoune Heights. The Sapoune Heights rose about seven hundred feet above the Balaclava

Redoubts, or emplacements, similar to the ones used in this camp of the 4th Light Dragoons, were criticized for their ineffective locations and hasty construction.

Plain, to the north and west of both the North and South Valleys and overlooking both. Farther west, beyond the ridge of the Sapoune Heights, lay the highlands called the Chersonese Heights. It was here, with their backs to Balaclava, that the British army laid siege to Sebastopol.

British Cavalry Units Based at Foot of Sapoune Heights

Because the British infantry was engaged in siege works, Lord Raglan assigned to his cavalry brigades part of the task of guarding the rear of the British army from the Balaclava Plain. The cavalry troops pitched their tents at the base of the Sapoune Heights, not far from the number six redoubt. From there they would act as overseers of the Balaclava Plain.

As the cavalry brigades stood with their backs to the Sapoune Heights, they could see rising before them the entire Balaclava Plain with the Causeway Heights running between the North and South Valleys. They also could see, rising to the north and west, another range of hills called the Fedioukine Heights. To the north of the Causeway Heights, on a slope of the Fedioukine Heights, lay a series of French entrenchments. These were manned by experienced French soldiers, some Zouaves, and several regiments of the Chasseurs d'Afrique along with some supporting artillery. All were under the command of General Bosquet, whom Russell describes as "a stout soldier like looking man, who reminds one of the old genre of French generals as depicted at Versailles."

Bosquet commanded two full divisions, most of whom were on the Chersonese Heights when the battle began. They were eager to descend to the plain and assist the British if called upon to do so.

The British cavalry brigades had with them a single troop of horse artillery to help protect against possible attacks from the Fedioukine Hills where, to the east of the French emplacements, the Russians had set up their own batteries under General Jaboritsky. The British horse artillery was under the command of Major Maude.

Anticipated Support of Infantry Units

The Highland Regiment and the Turks in the redoubts, as well as the cavalry, expected that if attacked, British infantry regiments from the Chersonese Heights behind them would immediately come to their rescue. In fact, these arrangements were based on the expectation of such support. Kinglake reports:

Our Engineers formed an entrenched position which could only have strength upon the supposition that several thousand of the Allied infantry would have time to come down and defend it . . . [otherwise] there was no good ground for imagining that the strength of this "outer line," or the prowess of the brave Osmanlis who were to be placed in its earthworks, could fairly be brought into use.

These arrangements constituted the entire defensive system that Lord Raglan prepared to protect his only source of supply from enemy attack. According to reporter Russell, "The position we occupied in reference to Balaclava was supposed by most people to be very strong—in fact impregnable."

Ominously, in late October, the allies became discouraged when they failed to capture Sebastopol quickly. On the other hand, Generals Menshikov and Gorchakov were optimistic that the Russians would enjoy an early victory. In addition, Menshikov knew that the tsar anxiously waited for news of such a Russian victory. Menshikov was a cautious man, but he also feared Nicholas's anger if the Russian army did not win a battle. Therefore, Menshikov decided to attack the British from the rear of their position.

The Russian general hid large units of infantry and cavalry in the hills behind the River Tchernaya and in the wooded areas that lie at the northern approach to the Balaclava Plain. He also had large numbers of troops based beyond the River Baidar to the east and in the Baidar valley beyond the river. Those Russian forces, less than three miles from Balaclava, were ordered "to keep a watch on the Tatar population [local people] and prevent it from taking provisions to the enemy."

Size of the Opposing Forces at Balaclava

By the time all his reinforcements arrived (on foot) from Bessarabia, Menshikov's total Russian strength in the area around Sebastopol numbered between eighty-five thousand and ninety thousand men. The allies had only eighty thousand troops. At the Battle of Balaclava perhaps twenty-five thousand Russian soldiers took part in the various actions. The allies could muster perhaps five thousand men.

Fortunately for the allies, Menshikov had a vacillating, negative nature. Despite his numerical superiority, in his heart he did not wish to fight. According to historian Albert Seaton, one of Menshikov's officers, Mitiutin, believed

> it was apparent that the Commander-in-Chief regarded the situation with the greatest of pessimism and despaired holding on to Sebastopol. But the sovereign [Nicholas I] would not entertain the thought of giving it up.

Forced into action, Menshikov entrusted the attack on Balaclava to his cavalry general, Pavel Liprandi. As Russell had anticipated,

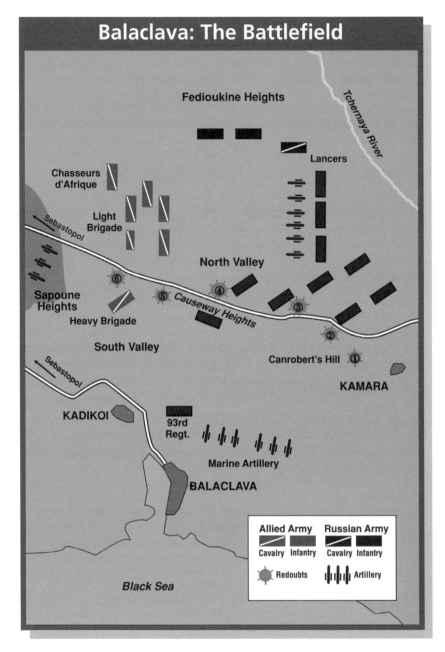

Balaclava: The Battlefield

Fedioukine Heights

Tchernaya River

Chasseurs d'Afrique

Lancers

Light Brigade

Sebastopol

North Valley

Sapoune Heights

Heavy Brigade

⑥

⑤

④

③

Causeway Heights

②

South Valley

Canrobert's Hill ①

Sebastopol

KAMARA

KADIKOI

93rd Regt.

Marine Artillery

BALACLAVA

Allied Army

Cavalry Infantry

Russian Army

Cavalry Infantry

Redoubts

Artillery

Black Sea

Liprandi prepared most of his men in the area around Chorgun, which lies beyond the Tchernaya River. The Russian army consisted of twenty-five infantry battalions, thirty-four cavalry squadrons, and seventy-eight guns.

Early on the morning of October 25, 1854, the Russians moved through the gaps and the gorges in the mountains and began their attack on the perimeter of the British position. The first of the four actions of the Battle of Balaclava, the attack on the redoubts, had begun.

CHAPTER FOUR

Attack on the Redoubts

The unskillful measures taken by the English Commander-in-Chief naturally could not fail to contribute to the success of the Russian arms. Lord Raglan had, in fact, established a vast entrenched camp, which was by no means in proportion with the number of his troops, destined at the same time to carry on the siege of Sebastopol, to cover the ridge of hills between Inkerman and Balaklava, and finally to defend the latter town itself.

General Todleben, quoted in
General Todleben's History of the Defense of Sebastopol

During the siege and bombardment of Sebastopol, General Menshikov sent out a number of spy missions to measure the strength of the British positions defending Balaclava. His patrols brought back very interesting information. They suggested that the outer defenses guarding the harbor were weakly held. In addition, the Russian patrols found only thin lines of enemy pickets, guards stationed beyond the camp, to give alarm if the enemy approached. These men were posted beyond the redoubts and close to the mountain passes behind which the Russians were building their strength. Some also were posted in an abandoned monastery facing the Baidar River.

The British pickets were next to useless. The patrols discovered them sleeping but did not kill them because at the time the Russians did not want their presence so near Balaclava to become known.

The information provided by the patrols convinced General Menshikov that he should plan to attack the British from behind.

He reasoned that an attack from the rear would force the British to remove some of their troops from the close siege on the Russian port. This withdrawal would reduce enemy pressure on Sebastopol, and if he were lucky, the attack might even drive the British from Balaclava.

British Aware of Russian Reconnaissance of Their Positions

Despite Russian precautions, the British High Command as well as the newspapermen with the British forces were aware of Menshikov's missions. William Howard Russell described these activities:

> It was evident enough that Menshikov and Gorchakov had been feeling their way along this route for several days past, and very probably at night the Cossacks had crept up close to our picquets, which are not always as watchful as might be desired, and had observed the weakness of a position far too extended for our army to defend, and occupied by their despised enemy, the Turks.

Nevertheless, in mid-October many people in the British army still did not take the Russian military threat as seriously as they soon would. For example, Daniel Lysons, a British soldier engaged in trenching work in front of Sebastopol, expressed his own high confidence regarding British military strength in a letter he wrote to his mother on October 12, 1854:

After learning about the weak British defenses at the port of Balaclava, Russian general Menshikov formulated his plan of attack. Menshikov hoped his plan would draw the British away from their siege of Sebastopol.

We have skirmishes occasionally on all sides; but the Russians have been so completely cowed by Alma, that I really believe a sergeant's guard might oppose a whole division. I have not the slightest doubts as to the results of the affair; whether I shall live through it is another thing. But Sebastopol will fall within a fortnight.

British Reluctance to Use Spies

In part this enthusiasm stemmed from the fact that the British had no idea how strong the Russian position was. Lord Raglan did not like to use spies, and he did not trust the information they provided. In fact, Raglan considered it unworthy of an English gentleman to have dealings with spies. According to Kinglake, "The gathering of knowledge by clandestine means was repulsive to the feeling of an English gentleman."

This attitude on the part of the British commander handicapped the British war effort. Two weeks before the Battle of Balaclava, Tatar spies, who had no love of the Russian conquerors of their Crimean homeland, brought news of large enemy buildups behind the Tchernaya River as well as behind the Baidar Valley, farther to the east.

In any event concealing the presence of an army growing to twenty-five thousand men was extremely difficult. In addition, it was not clear that the Russians wanted their presence concealed. However, according to C. E. Vulliamy, "Lord Raglan did not think it worth while to keep himself informed of those movements by close daily observation."

In early October British pickets near the village of Kamara did report to headquarters that they had observed several Russian infantry divisions crossing the Tchernaya River. The pickets even reported hearing military music accompanying the marchers. The buildup of the Russian army near Balaclava continued right up to the moment the battle began.

Warning of October 21, 1854

Finally, in the face of apparently large enemy troop concentrations near Kamara, Lord Raglan responded to some new and alarming information provided by Tatar spies. On October 21 Lord Raglan ordered one of his infantry generals, Sir George Cathcart, to move one thousand men of his Fourth Division from the Chersonese Heights to the Balaclava Plain. They were ordered to be on alert to support an anticipated attack on the outposts guarding the approaches to Balaclava.

The rumors of the Russian attack were premature. The Russians did not appear on the twenty-first. Raglan was angered by

Espionage as an Element in Warfare

For thousands of years army commanders have used spies to learn the intentions of their enemies. Romans and Greeks, Normans and French, English and Germans—all have taken advantage of secret information to increase the ability of their armies to defeat opposing forces. Certainly General George Washington used an entire, far-flung network of spies to determine the movement of the large and powerful British forces during the American Revolution.

During the Crimean War the Russian High Command frequently sent English- and French-speaking Russian spies into the camps of the allied armies to obtain information regarding the numerical strength and the health of the enemy troops. However, in the English army, Lord Raglan refused to use spies. He considered the practice beneath his dignity and beneath the dignity of his government. Only occasionally did he even use information that was obtained from captured enemy soldiers to strengthen or to change the position of his troops.

Consequently, General Raglan was completely unaware that twenty-five thousand Russian troops under the command of General Liprandi were assembled near the mountains beyond the Balaclava Plain. He ignored information supplied by Turkish spies and did not even send out his own pickets to determine the size or disposition of the enemy forces that the Turkish spies had located. The sheer bravery and determination of the British forces during the battle and the failure of the Russian leadership to take advantage of their own overwhelming power saved the British army from total defeat that day.

having ordered the needless and exhausting descent of General Cathcart's troops to the plain. General Cathcart himself was furious at what he saw as the unnecessary disturbance of his own routine. In addition, unfortunately, one British officer died of exposure, waiting on that cold fall night for the order to attack that never came. A good deal of grumbling passed between Raglan and Cathcart.

Disgustedly, Sir George Cathcart brought his cold and weary men back to their camp on the heights above the plain. Raglan determined not to send his infantry down again unless he learned that an attack actually was taking place.

Warning of Impending Attack Ignored

Therefore, when on October 24 a spy provided what turned out to be an accurate report of enemy troop movements, the British High Command did not take the report seriously. The information on October 24 came from a Turkish spy whom Rustem Pasha, a Turkish officer and one of the leaders of the Turkish forces at Balaclava, had sent into the hills behind the Tchernaya River.

The spy obtained amazingly accurate information. He identified Pavel Liprandi as the officer in charge of the forces poised to attack Balaclava. With great accuracy, he also told Rustem Pasha that about twenty-five thousand Russian troops, consisting of cavalry, infantry, and artillery units, were preparing for battle and that the attack would come from at least three different directions.

Hurriedly, Rustem Pasha sent the information to Lord Lucan, commander of the cavalry division, and to Sir Colin Campbell, who was the officer in charge of the Ninety-third Highlanders. Both men spoke with the spy and came to the conclusion that his information was accurate. Lucan sent his aide-de-camp, his son Lord Bingham, to British headquarters to alert Lord Raglan to the immediate danger threatening his rear position.

Lord Bingham could not get an interview with Lord Raglan. Instead, he passed along the urgent message to Raglan's quartermaster general, General Sir Richard Airey. Airey himself took the warning to Raglan. Lord Raglan read the message, dismissed it with what Vulliamy calls "a curt reply, 'Very Well!,'" and did not bother to acknowledge its receipt to Lucan and Campbell.

Russian Forces Attacking the Redoubts

The warning Raglan dismissed referred to the force that the Russians designated the Detachment of Tchorgoun. It was divided into three separate units, one commanded by General Gribbe, a second by General Semiakine, and the third by Colonel Scudery. A separate detachment, commanded by General Jaboritsky, had orders to cooperate with Liprandi and his three subordinates. Jaboritsky's forces positioned themselves on the Fedioukine Heights to the north of the North Valley and east of the position occupied by the French.

British pickets as usual had been posted the night of October 24, in several positions beyond the redoubts, but they had not been alert enough to warn of the attack. Fortunately, the alertness of the field officer of the day saved the pickets from capture by the Russians. The officer, out on his rounds, discovered that the Russians were advancing. He rode out to the line of pickets and alerted them in time for them to escape.

Meanwhile, the Russian armies struck at the redoubts shortly after five o'clock in the morning of October 25. Fewer than two thousand men prepared to defend themselves against a possible enemy force of twenty-five thousand, at least ten thousand of whom struck the redoubts from three separate directions. Cavalry and infantry columns led by skirmishers, skilled riflemen sent out in front of the main body of soldiers, poured onto the plain from their concealed camps in the mountains and rushed toward the redoubts. The answering fire from Turkish muskets and naval guns in the redoubts shattered the predawn silence of the Balaclava Plain.

The Role of Russian Spies in the Crimean War

Because British army officers disdained the use of spies, they often found themselves under attack without warning. Historian Christopher Hibbert in *The Destruction of Lord Raglan: A Tragedy of the Crimean War* describes how the Russians obtained useful information regarding the size and strength of British forces.

The British headquarters, following the lead of Lord Raglan's known prejudice, did not like making use of spies. The Russians, more realistically, had no such old-fashioned scruples. Enemy officers wearing British uniforms were on several occasions discovered inspecting the French trenches; and men in French uniforms frequently wandered through the British lines and then scampered back into Sebastopol. One day a friendly-looking man wearing civilian clothes walked into a gun battery and said he was a surgeon. He asked several questions in a Yorkshire accent and then inquired the best way to the forward trenches. He was seen a little later running headlong for Sebastopol. British intelligence, on the other hand, was mainly confined to the conflicting and unreliable information of Russian deserters, mainly all Poles, and to the often misleading reports of Turkish spies.

High Command Unaware That Battle Is Under Way

In this first action of the Battle of Balaclava, the Turks fought hard to defend their exposed positions and their lives. Their task was to delay the Russians until the British awoke to the danger and came to their assistance. However, the British High Command up on the Sapoune Heights was at first completely unaware that the battle had begun. In addition, Lord Cardigan, commander of the Light Brigade, was asleep on his yacht in the harbor and would not wake up for another three hours.

Only Lord Lucan, the cavalry commander, and Sir Colin Campbell, commander of the Highlanders, were uneasy that morning and sensed the danger to the British position. Shortly before the Russians attacked the redoubts, Lord Lucan had aroused the cavalry and kept the troopers at the ready at the base of the Sapoune Heights. He was so anxious that they be prepared for battle that the horses were not watered and the men did not have time for breakfast.

Then Lucan, accompanied by two members of his staff, Sir George Paget and Major McMahon, rode out to patrol the Causeway Heights. Feathery mist lay lightly on the hilltops before him.

The air was chilly but calm. He was soon joined on the causeway by Sir Colin Campbell, who had come up from his own camp before Balaclava to review the advance Turkish positions.

Lord Lucan Learns of Russian Attack

The small group was within three hundred paces of Canrobert's Hill when the men suddenly halted. All four were shocked by the sight ahead of them. By the first light of dawn, Sir George Paget saw that two flags, not one, flew from the number one redoubt, Canrobert's Hill. Two flags signaled that the enemy at that very moment was advancing on the position. Moments later the first sound of gunfire confirmed that the Russians were attacking the redoubts.

Sir Colin Campbell and Lord Lucan agreed that this time the Russian attack was not like what historian John Sweetman called the "nuisance pinprick raid" that had so annoyed Lord Raglan on October 21. The British horsemen quickly took action. The cavalrymen rushed back to the British encampment. A trumpeter sounded the alarm for the Heavy Brigade to mount up for action. Sir George Paget galloped back to ready the Light Brigade. Sir Colin Campbell made preparations to defend against an attack on the port. Lord Lucan sent Captain Charteris, one of his aides, up to the Sapoune Heights to warn General Raglan that the vulnerable rear position of the British army was under attack.

The British cavalry charges into action at the Battle of Balaclava.

As the sun began to rise above the plain, these British officers had great hopes for success. After all, that Wednesday, October 25, 1854, was the 439th anniversary of St. Crispin's Day, the holiday that commemorates King Henry V of England's great victory over the French at Agincourt.

Unfortunately, the Turks defending Canrobert's Hill and the other redoubts quickly lost all illusions regarding their own fate. The redoubts lay between a mile and two and a half miles from the nearest possible allied support. The British cavalry and Captain Maude's six-gun mounted artillery supplied all the assistance the British could lend to the Turks at the moment. The Turks, however, knew that the cavalry in general, unsupported by infantry, most likely would not take on the hordes of Russians sweeping toward them. In fact, during this first phase of the battle "Lucan led the Heavies back east with no intent to engage the Russians but flamboyantly maneuvered the brigade, hoping to dissuade the Russian advance" by tempting them away from the redoubts. These efforts were futile. In the end, the British cavalry did not come to the support of the Turks.

The British mounted artillery force did fire its guns at the Russian troops attacking the redoubts, but were soon forced to withdraw. Maude, in charge of the horse artillery, was terribly wounded during this action when a shell shattered the insides of his horse and then raked his own body. The six British guns quickly ran out of ammunition. Once the British supply of shells was exhausted, Lord Lucan ordered the horse artillery to withdraw from the battlefield. Thereafter, the horse artillery rendered little service to the Turks.

Lord Raglan eventually issued orders for two of his infantry divisions to begin to descend from the Chersonese Heights to the Balaclava Plain. Unfortunately, the fate of the redoubts and of their Turkish defenders would be settled long before the arrival of those infantry divisions many hours later.

Attack on Canrobert's Hill

The Russians began their attack on Canrobert's Hill, the most remote of the redoubts, by hurling against it large numbers of riflemen who ran in front of huge gray columns of infantry and cavalry. The Russians tried to rush the walls of Canrobert's Hill, but the six hundred Turks, assisted by their three 12-pound naval guns, rebuffed the first wave of Russians with a storm of musket fire.

Successive waves of overwhelmingly huge numbers of Russians continued to assault the poorly constructed earthworks. The thirty Russian guns on the Kamara hills soon silenced the Turkish fieldpieces and destroyed much of the sheltered space within the redoubt.

The surviving Turks withdrew from the exposed portion of Canrobert's Hill to the more protected southern portion of the redoubt and continued to fire upon the Russians. Russians climbing up the walls protected themselves by using thorn scrub and bushes as cover. Finally, a little past seven o'clock in the morning, after more than one and a half hours of furious battle, the Russians overwhelmed the small band of Turkish defenders.

At that point, units of the regiment made up of men from the town of Azoff, led by Colonel Kridener, raced across the ditch that surrounded the redoubt and rushed over the crumbling ramparts. The surviving Turkish soldiers fled to the rear of the redoubt to make a last heroic stand. Kinglake describes the scene:

> The many flooded in upon the few, overwhelming, surrounding, destroying, yet still confronted with heroic desperation, and owing all the way they could make to the sheer fighting of the men, who thus closed with their Musselman foe, and to the weight of the numbers behind them.

Many Turks were sabered by the Russian cavalry. Finally, realizing that no assistance would come to them, the Turks abandoned their position and the bodies of 170 dead comrades to rush over the south wall of the redoubt and run for their lives toward the relative safety of the harbor. By 7:30 the Azoff regiment proudly planted its standard on the top of the redoubt.

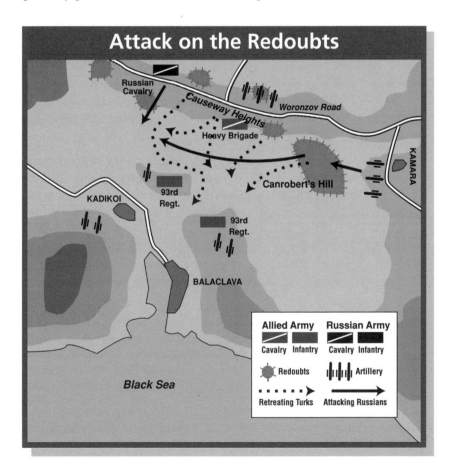

Attack on the Redoubts

Russian Cavalry

Causeway Heights

Woronzov Road

Heavy Brigade

Canrobert's Hill

KAMARA

93rd Regt.

KADIKOI

93rd Regt.

BALACLAVA

Black Sea

Allied Army **Russian Army**
Cavalry Infantry   Cavalry Infantry

⚙ Redoubts   ‖‖‖ Artillery

• • • • ▶   ⟶
Retreating Turks   Attacking Russians

Fall of Canrobert's Hill Demoralizes Defenders of Other Redoubts

The lesson of the fall of Canrobert's Hill was not lost on the defenders of redoubts two, three, and four. Three Ukraine battalions and four battalions of the Odessa regiment now advanced upon the smaller redoubts. The fifteen hundred British cavalrymen still made no effort to assist them. When the remaining Turks saw their fellow troopers abandoning Canrobert's Hill, they, too, rushed over the southern walls of their own redoubts and ran toward the port. The Russian cavalry followed them and sabered many Turks in the back as they ran for their lives.

As a result of this action, the Russians gained possession of nine 12-pound naval guns that had defended the redoubts. They then turned the guns toward the south and fired on the fleeing Turks.

British and French commanders, along with several reporters, watched the attack on the Turks in the redoubts from the safety of the heights above the valley. Now they saw the folly of their inferior defenses. The Turks had bravely attempted to hold their position despite the overwhelming odds and the failure of the British to come to their assistance. The marquess of Anglesey calls the Turkish action that day "an heroic resistance which gave the allies more than an hour's invaluable breathing space."

Some observers on the Sapoune Heights thought otherwise. When the Turks finally succumbed and ran for their lives, British observers condemned them as cowards. Reporter William Howard Russell strongly reflected this condescending attitude toward the Turks in his dispatches back to London. The dispatch he sent on the evening of the battle is typical of this attitude:

> All the stories we had heard about their bravery behind stone walls and earthen works proved how differently the same or similar people fight under different circumstances. When the Russians advanced, the Turks fired a few rounds at them, got frightened at the distance of their support in the rear, looked round, received a few shots and shell and then bolted and fled with an agility quite at variance with common-place notions of Oriental deportment on the battlefield.

The failure of the Turks to hold the redoubts posed a terrible strategic problem. The loss considerably reduced the strength of the already weak British defensive position near the entrance to the port of Balaclava. Certainly, the British position was far more precarious than it had been two hours earlier.

At 7:30 that crisp October morning, the Russians had in their possession the additional nine fieldpieces they had captured from the Turks, the large battery of field guns they emplaced several days earlier on the Kamara Heights, and the ammunition

Media Coverage of the Battle of Balaclava

Newspapermen stood on the Sapoune Heights on the morning of October 25, 1854, as the Battle of Balaclava unfolded on the plain below. Their presence marked the very first time in history that newspapers had sent reporters and sometimes even people skilled in the new technique of photography into battle with the troops.

The most important war reporter was the black-bearded, outspoken, and very talented writer William Howard Russell. Russell's long, well-written, dramatic, and bloody accounts familiarized the British public with the events of the war. Thus Russell can be considered to be the very first war correspondent. He obtained information that rarely appeared in the official reports sent back by the general officers in the field. They certainly did not want the War Department in London to know about their incompetence as military leaders.

Russell reported openly on whatever he saw and heard. He recorded the agony of the soldiers who died from cholera, dysentery, exposure, and lack of care. He wrote about the terrible food and lack of clothing and shelter. In particular he wrote about the amazing bravery and dedication of the British common soldiers and about the deplorable lack of military ability displayed by the British generals. Russell told the English public in great detail what he saw on October 25, 1854.

Because Russell watched the Battle of Balaclava from the top of the heights, he was able to see the changing events of the day far better than the generals on the field. In particular, he saw and was outraged by the blunders committed by Lord Lucan and Lord Cardigan. He told the English public that the blunders of these officers led to the destruction of the Light Brigade.

The living conditions, the treatment of the British soldiers by their officers, and the stupidity displayed by many of them during the Crimean War were no worse than the horrors that British soldiers had endured in earlier wars. However, Russell made the British public aware of how their brave men were mistreated and how poorly they were led by nonprofessional, untrained officers. Russell's reports and the public indignation they aroused led to the recall of Lord Lucan and Lord Cardigan. The reports also contributed greatly to the massive reforms in all the branches of the British military system that began almost immediately after the war ended.

British journalist William Howard Russell, known for his frank reports on the Crimean War, writes a dispatch in his tent. In the background, Florence Nightingale waits to receive wounded soldiers.

that they could turn on the British. The Russians also had control of the strategically important Causeway Heights. The Russians now represented a significant threat to the British control of its port and its facilities.

The Russian army was buoyed by its success. It could now turn its attention to the tiny force of British troops that defended the entrance to the port of Balaclava. After 7:30 that morning, the Russians prepared to advance on the port. If the British defensive forces failed to hold, Balaclava surely was lost. The first phase of the Battle of Balaclava was over. The second was about to begin.

CHAPTER FIVE

The Attack on the Port

The Russians charged toward Balaclava. The ground flew beneath the horses' feet: gathering speed at every stride they dashed on towards that thin red line tipped with steel.

William Howard Russell, October 25, 1854

The Russian cavalry tasted victory as the gray-clad horsemen followed and slaughtered many of the Turkish soldiers who fled in terror from the redoubts. The *Times* reporter observed the scene in horror; the rush of the Russian cavalry seemed unstoppable:

The solid column of cavalry opens like a fan, and resolves itself into a long spray of skirmishers. It laps the flying Turks, steel flashes in the air, and down go the poor Moslems quivering on the plain, split through fez and musket guard to the chin and breast-belt. There is no support for them.

After overriding the fleeing Turks, the Russian cavalry intended to destroy whatever defenses lay between itself and the port of Balaclava. If the port fell, the British position would become indefensible.

The Ninety-third Highlanders defended the entrance to the port. Looking splendid in their traditional bright red jackets and kilts, the unit prepared to face the oncoming Russian cavalry.

When the first phase of the Battle of Balaclava began, the Highlanders had taken up a position not too distant from the redoubts. Consequently, when the Russians overran the redoubts, they turned the captured naval guns onto the Highlanders causing

Sir Colin Campbell, experienced and skilled in battle but lacking the rank of a noble, led the Ninety-third Highlanders during the defense of the Balaclava Plain.

several casualties. Sir Colin Campbell ordered his Highlanders to move back to a safer position beyond the hillock, which later came to be called the Sutherland Hillock. There they began to wait for the right moment to strike against their Russian enemies.

On that day, through a most unusual set of circumstances, Sir Colin Campbell, although not noble by birth, had overall command of the Highlanders on the plain. By merit he deserved the position. Although Sir Colin was Lord Lucan's junior in rank, Campbell was his superior in ability and professional experience. He was a career officer who had served under both Moore and Wellington during the Napoleonic wars. Since then he had seen service in Spain, in America during the War of 1812, and later in China. He displayed brilliant leadership during the Second Sekh War (1846–1848).

Nonetheless, after forty-four years of outstanding service for the British government, Colin Campbell was still only a colonel. Unlike many noblemen with titles of general who took part in the battle that day, Campbell did not have the background, money, or political connections to purchase a higher rank.

Although Campbell did not command a division, he distinguished himself at the Battle of the Alma and impressed Lord Raglan with his ability to control his men in battle. As Lord Raglan became increasingly angered and frustrated by the constant feuding between Lords Cardigan and Lucan, he lost faith in the ability of either man to deal with difficult situations. Fortunately for the British army, Lord Raglan recognized Campbell's ability to lead men in battle. In the words of Captain Maude of the horse artillery attached to the cavalry brigades, "Lord Raglan would not trust Lord Lucan to defend Balaclava, so he sent down Sir Colin Campbell." Raglan placed Colin Campbell in command of the defenses of Balaclava, leapfrogging him over Lord Lucan, who by rank should have had total command of the British position on the Balaclava Plain and of all the men who defended it.

Lucan and Campbell Work Well Together

The situation was far from perfect. The actual defenses of Balaclava were now divided between a cavalry general and an infantry officer, and Lord Raglan would permit neither to command the forces of the other. Fortunately for the British army, Lucan continued to remain on excellent terms with Campbell. Lucan readily agreed to Campbell's decision two days before the battle to set up a twelve-hundred-man marine artillery encampment above Kadikoi.

So Campbell called Lieutenant Roberts of the Royal Marine Artillery to his side. Roberts later wrote that "on the evening of the 23rd, Sir Colin Campbell sent for me and asked me like a good boy to go up the hill and superintend the formation of a battery of three guns for the sake of an old fellow who had a great deal of responsibility on his shoulders." When the attack came, these guns were in position on the high ground above the port facing the oncoming Russian cavalrymen.

Campbell Studies the Plain of Balaclava

The following evening, Campbell and Lord George Paget of the Light Brigade took a walk out on the ridge above the port and then into the North Valley to see if they could detect signs or sounds of Russian troop movements. Paget later wrote that Sir Colin, despite his sixty-one years, got down on the ground and put his ear against the earth to see if he could detect the sound of enemy horse movements.

Before dawn on October 25, Campbell rode up from Kadikoi and conferred with Lord Lucan. The two men agreed that the attack on the redoubts represented the opening phase of a full-scale attack on the British position. Sir Colin suggested to Lucan that, based on the direction of the Russian assault, Lucan place the Heavy Brigade in the South Valley, opposite redoubts four and five.

Accordingly, Lord Lucan positioned the Heavy Brigade across the valley so that his cavalry faced eastward. If the Russian cavalry then tried to attack near the approach to the port, its right flank would be exposed to Lucan's forces.

This coordinated arrangement, if successful, would effectively reduce the strength and force of the Russian cavalry charge. A coordinated plan had an advantage over the Russian units, which operated independently of one another, and followed outdated instructions that General Menshikov had issued to them hours or even days earlier.

Unfortunately, Lord Raglan, observing the battlefield from the Sapoune Heights, decided to alter the plans of Lucan and Campbell. Although he had no field experience and did not understand the objectives of his officers, Raglan decided that he did not want the Heavy Brigade to act without the assistance of a large infantry force. Raglan sent Captain Wetherall, one of his aides, with an order to Lucan to change his position. The order read: "Cavalry to take ground to the left of second line of redoubts occupied." Apparently Lucan, whose reputation already had been called into question—he was known as "Lord Look-On" because he did not appear ever to take the initiative—showed some resentment at the order to withdraw yet another time. Captain Wetherall remained with Lucan until the order had been carried out according to Lord Raglan's intentions.

Meanwhile Raglan issued orders to General Sir George Cathcart and to the duke of Cambridge to prepare the Fourth and the First Divisions, respectively, to descend to the plain. While the duke of Cambridge slowly prepared his division for the descent, General Cathcart did not. He was still indignant over having been asked to move his forces in response to a false alarm on October 21. Cathcart allowed his men to have breakfast rather than obey orders to descend immediately to the plain. As a result, Cathcart's division did not arrive on the field of battle until after all action had been completed, at about 10:30 in the morning.

In effect, Lord Raglan had overruled the coordinated plans of Sir Colin Campbell and Lord Lucan, plans that might have diminished the force of the Russian cavalry attack. Raglan's infantry divisions were slow to get into a supporting position. Consequently, the British interior defenses of the port were in an extremely precarious position. The Highlanders were left almost entirely on their own to face however many of his twenty-five thousand available troopers General Liprandi decided to send against them.

A change in orders forced the Highlanders to defend the port of Balaclava without the aid of Lucan's cavalry.

Small Force Under Command of Campbell

Campbell's forces certainly were quite meager under the circumstances. The central corps of his troops consisted of approximately 450 Sutherland Highlanders of the Ninety-third Regiment, under the immediate command of Colonel Ainslie. These Highlanders were soon joined by about 100 wounded and ill troopers under the command of Colonel Daveney. These soldiers, survivors of the trenches at Sebastopol, had been sent to Balaclava to recover from their wounds or illness. In the face of imminent danger, however, these men dragged themselves out of their sickbeds to stand alongside the Highlanders during the Russian attack.

Major Gorden, who commanded two companies of the Highlanders and had been on duty elsewhere, hurried to join Campbell before the attack began. Finally, several groups of Turkish soldiers also joined forces with the Highlanders. Some had been on harbor duty, and Campbell placed

Arrogance of the Nonprofessional Soldier

In *The Invasion of the Crimea*, Kinglake preserves for posterity the exchange between General Cathcart and Lord Raglan's messenger who urged him to hurry his troops down to the Balaclava Plain on the morning of October 25. Raglan's staff officer ordered George Cathcart to move immediately to the assistance of the Turks. In such circumstances the word of the staff officer was the equivalent of a direct order from Lord Raglan. Cathcart told him that it was

> "Quite impossible, sir for the 4th Division to move."

The staff officer replied:

> "My orders were very positive, and the Russians are advancing upon Balaclava."

Cathcart replied:

> "I can't help that sir, it is impossible for my Division to move, as the greater portion of the men have only just come from the trenches. The best thing you can do is to sit down and take some breakfast with me."

A short time later some bugles sounded and the division began its slow descent to the Balaclava Plain.

British general George Cathcart disregarded the order to move his division to the Balaclava Plain until after he and his troops had breakfast.

them on the right wing of his group. Many others were survivors of the attack on the redoubts. Captain Tatham, the senior naval officer in the harbor, met the Turks as they ran toward Kadikoi. He had climbed the road to where the Highlanders were established near Kadikoi. Although Tatham knew no Turkish, he was able to rally the fleeing Turks. Tatham formed the Turks into two lines and placed them on the left wing of the Highlanders.

This small, stalwart force stood prepared to protect the port against a huge horde of Russian cavalry. They were all that separated the Russians from the British army's source of supplies in the harbor and its small arsenal at Kadikoi.

Ordinarily an infantry unit preparing to face a cavalry charge forms into a hollow square. Campbell, however, arranged his men in two lines, perhaps in an effort to increase the length of the line of defense before the road leading to the harbor. Campbell's unit awaited the Russian cavalry attack from a position south of the number four redoubt, which the Turks had just abandoned, and somewhat to the north of Kadikoi.

At that moment Russian cavalry general Pavel Liprandi enjoyed sole command of the plain, but he displayed a curious reluctance to press on and take advantage of the situation. Although the attack on the redoubts had given him a victory, a Turkish banner of war, and British naval guns, Liprandi may have suspected that the British had set a trap for his forces. Whatever his reasons, Liprandi hesitated before moving forward. This pause enabled Campbell to rally his men, give them instructions, and line them up in preparation for the attack.

The Russian Cavalry Attack

Finally Liprandi ordered part of the Russian cavalry under General Ryzhov into the North Valley. Meanwhile a smaller force of Ryzhov's command, several Cossack squadrons from the Don region, fourteen squadrons of the Kievsky and Ingermanlandsky hussars, and two horse artillery troops—perhaps four hundred horsemen in all—began the approach toward the Highland Scots of the Ninety-third Regiment. The Russians understood their instructions. They were to attack the British infantry near Kadikoi. They also were directed to destroy an artillery depot that General Menshikov believed lay concealed near Kadikoi. If Balaclava also fell, they would enjoy a great victory indeed.

The Russian cavalry approached the crest of Sutherland Hill and prepared to attack. Russell reports there was a moment of silence, broken only by "the champing of bits and clink of sabres in the valley." Then the Russians charged the Highlanders who had just moved behind Sutherland Hill to the east of the number four redoubt.

Campbell later wrote a dispatch to Major General Estcourt of General Raglan's staff in which he explained the temporary withdrawal of his men from the crest of the hill to a position slightly behind it. He wanted to protect his men from shell fire.

> [He] made them retire a few paces behind the crest of the hill. During this period our batteries on the heights, manned by the Royal Marine Artillery and the Royal Marines, made excellent practice on the enemy's Cavalry which came over the hill in our front.

The Highlanders lay down in the grass, eagerly awaiting the order to stand and fire.

Campbell Controls Enthusiasm of His Troops

Campbell knew his men were impatient to meet the enemy. He later wrote:

> Here they lay, impatient in the grass, and when it was known that the mass of enemy cavalry was approaching, they sprang up, lining the crest of the hill and evidently preparing for a charge. Their guns trained expectantly, gunners waiting for the word; a shuffling and murmur betrayed the grim patience of the ranks.

This took place when the Russians were about one thousand yards from the British troops. Todleben, who wrote a history of these events, indicates that the Highlanders were such disciplined soldiers that they "allowed the Hussars to approach within musket shot of them before they fired."

Second Retreat of the Turks

At about this time, most of the Turks on either side of the Highlanders fired a round at the oncoming Russians and then fled toward the harbor in terror. The recent death of so many of their comrades in the redoubts and their lack of training made them incapable of facing the charging Russian cavalry. Campbell later reported that the terrified Turks ran to Balaclava, crying "ship, ship" as they tried to reach the safety of the port.

Campbell had suddenly lost a third of his forces, but he did not lose his courage or his control over the Highlanders. Sir Colin Campbell rode along the line of the Highlanders. In the moments before the Russians charged, he told his men: "Remember, there is no retreat from here. You must die where you stand." The historian Kinglake recorded the response of Campbell's men. Major Burroughs, officer in command of the sixth company of the Ninety-third Highland Regiment, cheerily answered his appeal saying "Ay, ay, Sir Colin, we'll do that."

The Russian cavalry drew nearer. Campbell ordered his men to stand and hurry to the top of the little hill behind which they had been protecting themselves. Their excitement was electric as they prepared to meet the cavalry. Campbell sensed that his men wanted to charge the oncoming cavalry. He turned in his saddle and shouted at them: "93rd! 93rd! Damn all that eagerness!"

The Russian charge against the Highlanders came closer. The awesome sight inspired Russell, watching from the Sapoune Heights, to write about the "thin red streak topped with a line of steel." Soon those words would be abbreviated to "that thin red line." The words stuck, and ever since that time, the phrase has been associated with the bravery of the gallant Ninety-third Highland Regiment.

Indeed, that thin red line of tartan-tweeded Highlanders held steady. At six hundred yards, the distance between themselves and the charging Russian cavalry still was too great for their guns to be effective. Nevertheless, the Highlanders, so few in number and many of them already mortally ill from dysentery and cholera, fired a volley that created a good deal of smoke but few casualties.

At one hundred and fifty yards, the Highlanders fired another volley. This time the bullets fired from the Highlanders' Minié rifles hit their marks, and many Russians fell to the ground. The Russian frontal attack had not destroyed the two lines of British soldiers, so the Russian commander changed his strategy. The Russians tried to turn to their own left in an effort to attack the British on their weaker right side.

Campbell had experienced similar changes in strategy during his long career, and he knew how to respond. He ordered the grenadier company on the right line to "bring the left shoulder forward, and show a front towards the north-east" while they kept up their firing. Campbell's quick response effectively stopped the Russians from continuing their assault on the Highlanders. Instead, the British were able to fire upon the Russians' exposed flank.

Retreat of Russian Cavalry

The Ninety-third Highlanders, called "that thin red line," were few in number but effective on the battlefield.

There was more gunfire, and more Russians fell; finally, the Russian cavalry under Ryzhov's command turned, wheeled again to

Battle Spectators

Onlookers, safe on the bluffs overlooking the plain of Balaclava, watch as the battle rages on.

While the Battle of Balaclava developed on the plain below the heights, spectators experienced something like watching a modern movie set. The spectators were safe from dangerous military actions, and they had refreshments to keep them comfortable. In his book *Crimea*, C. E. Vulliamy captures something of the picniclike spirit of the morning.

> The row of spectators on the Sapoune Ridge, and there were many of them, let out an exulting cry of "Bravo, Highlanders!"—as if they had been the spectators of a glorious though bloody game.
>
> Nothing is more peculiar in the whole course of this peculiar battle, than the comfortable and advantageous position of those who were observing the encounters. They stood or sat, or ambled about on their horses, along the top of the great limestone bluff, looking down on the valleys and over the low hills. Here were Raglan, Canrobert, Bosquet; here were the staffs and the "hangers-on" and a crowd of "amateurs" and newspaper correspondents, including the famous Mr. Russell. These people, with binoculars or telescopes, were having a splendid view of the action, with all its alternations of misguided impetuosity and of bewildering pause, while they themselves were out of range and were able to sip their sherry and eat their sandwiches in the most enviable security.

the left, and retreated over the Causeway Heights to join the main body of Russian cavalry under the command of General Pavel Liprandi. The Highlanders sent yet another volley at the Russians fleeing across the South Valley. Unfortunately, the gunfire could not compensate for a cavalry charge on the Russian flank, which Lucan could have undertaken before Raglan countermanded the order.

Clearly, General Liprandi was embarrassed that British infantry units had driven off his cavalry. In his report the following day, he misrepresented the size of the enemy force he had faced. He told Menshikov that the Russian cavalry had been repulsed because it had been attacked by the British infantry on the flank and by the cavalry from the front.

The Highlanders themselves were joyous over the results of their action. A wild cheer rose from the throats of the Highlanders as the Russians rode away. The military and civilian spectators on the Sapoune Heights echoed the cheer. They had witnessed a unique act of bravery and appreciated the significance of what they had seen.

"Bravo, Highlanders! well done!" the spectators shouted. These same spectators were still eating their sandwiches, sipping their sherry, and applauding the bravery of the Highlanders and their commander when the third major event of the day, the Charge of the Heavy Brigade, began on the plain below.

CHAPTER SIX

The Charge of the Heavy Brigade

If a man has to hear that in the open forenoon of an October day a body of Russian horses which numbered itself by thousands could come wandering into the precincts of the English camp without exciting early attention on the part of our cavalry people, he ought to know what was the cause which made such an incident possible.

A. W. Kinglake, *The Invasion of the Crimea*

The third action of the Battle of Balaclava began in a most curious, almost accidental way. In response to Lord Raglan's orders, Lord Lucan already had the Heavy Brigade withdrawn from the area near the number five redoubt from which it could have supported the Ninety-third Highlanders. From its new position, the Heavy Brigade watched helplessly as the Russians overcame the redoubts and sent their hussars to attack the Highlanders who were defending the road leading to the port.

Lord Lucan was furious. He bitterly resented suggestions that he was a coward. He knew his inaction in the war was none of his doing. Lord Raglan himself had announced that he intended to keep the cavalry in a bandbox, that is, very safe and out of harm's way. They were very few in number, and Raglan wanted to use the cavalry judiciously. The cavalrymen wanted to gain military glory.

Lord Lucan as well as his hated brother-in-law, Lord Cardigan, expressed their bitterness and anger at their forced inaction in letters to friends in government in London. The correspondence produced governmental efforts to interfere with the conduct of the war.

This kind of mischief increased Raglan's own anxiety over how best to use his cavalry and increased the hostility between the two cavalry commanders. It also created dissension in the army and a fatal inclination on the part of the cavalry commanders to overreact when action by the cavalry was needed.

Delay in Receiving Instructions

Now, Lord Raglan, overlooking the action below, saw that the redoubts were about to fall and that Balaclava itself was under attack. So he sent an order to Lucan to come to the aid of the Turks and the Highlanders. By the time this order reached Lord Lucan about a half hour later, the redoubts had fallen and the Russian hussars had been driven back to the main body of Russian cavalry under General Ryzhov.

That great mass of Russian cavalry in gray field coats moved back and forth in the North Valley, just beyond the Causeway Heights. Then, just as the Heavy Brigade began to move east to provide belated assistance to a now nonexistent situation, the Russian cavalry moved up the Causeway Heights facing south. It crossed the crest of the heights and began its descent into the South Valley.

The British High Command watched the action in horror from above. To Raglan and his staff it appeared that the Russian cavalry would momentarily collide with the flank of the British Heavy Brigade under the command of General Sir James Scarlett. Such an unexpected attack on the British flank surely would destroy the Heavy Brigade.

Heavy Brigade Designed for Shock Tactics

The unit's name, Heavy Brigade, described its function as an extremely powerful thrusting machine. The horses of the brigade were larger, stronger, and heavier than those of the Light Brigade. They also stood several hands higher than the horses of the Russian cavalry with which they were about to collide.

One-on-one, the British cavalry troops enjoyed an advantage over their Russian counterparts. However, the British force of about 850 men was less than one-third the size of the cavalry force of approximately 3,000 Russian horsemen moving toward it.

In addition, the Russians were bearing down on the Heavies from higher ground. The two forces were as yet totally unaware of each other's presence. While Raglan could look down from his vantage of six hundred feet, the rise in the heights obscured the two cavalry forces from each other.

Lord Raglan had not bothered to inform Lord Lucan of the presence of the great mass of Russians in the North Valley. This failure is best explained by Lord Raglan's lack of military experience. He did not understand that the Balaclava Plain was not level. What Raglan saw from a height of six hundred feet above the sloping plains was not equally visible to the cavalry leaders. The result was that, according to historian John Selby, "Lord Raglan saw no reason to acquaint Lucan with the enemy's movement because he was quite unaware that Lucan could not see them himself."

As the Russians appeared over the rise, their much larger numbers and the advantage of the high ground they held placed the British in a terribly dangerous situation. The Russians could charge down the hill into the unprepared British Heavy Brigade, rout the English, and utterly destroy the outnumbered brigade.

Unaware of the danger that awaited it, the Heavy Brigade moved eastward along the south slope of the Causeway Heights. Suddenly, however, Lieutenant Alexander James Hardy Elliot, Scarlett's aide-de-camp, looked up toward his left. Sunlight reflected on the tips of the Russian lancer heads from the other side of the hill while the riders themselves still were concealed by it.

In an instant the British were alerted to the presence of their enemy. In response to Elliot's urgings, General Scarlett immediately altered his course. The Heavies began changing their line of march just as the first units of the Russian cavalry finally appeared at the crest of the hill and looked down on the 850 men of the Heavy Brigade.

Russell of the *Times*, among the crowd on the Sapoune Heights, recorded the moment for posterity: "The first line of Russian cavalry appeared to be at least double the length of ours—it was three times as deep. Behind them was a similar line, equally strong and compact." In fact, at this moment the observers on the heights and General Scarlett himself believed that a force of about three thousand Russians appeared to be preparing to attack the much inferior and poorly positioned Heavies.

Lord Raglan (pictured) was unaware that the Heavy Brigade could not see the great number of Russians assembling in the valley. Raglan's failure to warn Lord Lucan appeared to seal a dismal fate for the British.

Halt of Russian Cavalry on Crest of Causeway

Then suddenly, inexplicably, the Russians halted, just as they had halted momentarily before charging at the Ninety-third Highlanders before Balaclava. General Ryzhov evaluated the situation and then issued orders to his subordinates. Out from the center, moving to both left and right, two groups of Russian cavalry took up positions at the extremes of their line. The result was that the Russian front was extended on either side and covered the crest of the hill to a great distance beyond the line of the British cavalry. It appeared that the Russian cavalry was protected by the horns of a great bull.

The halt of the Russian cavalry and the time required to create its enveloping flanks gave General Scarlett just enough time to prepare his own troops for action. Like the Russian delay before Balaclava, Ryzhov's delay in attacking the Heavies was critically important to the British in the battle.

General Sir James Scarlett, like most of the British leaders, was new to warfare. The fifty-five-year-old general presented a dramatic military figure. His face matched the color of his name, and he wore huge white mustachios. More to the point, Scarlett had never before led a troop of cavalry into action. In fact, this was his very first military engagement. Unlike most senior British officers, however, Scarlett had common sense, good intuition, a keen understanding of his own deficiencies, and a willingness to make up for his shortcomings by taking advantage of the knowledge provided by his junior officers.

In fact, unlike most British senior officers, Scarlett chose men with field experience in India as his juniors. These men supplied the knowledge that Scarlett lacked, and he did not resent their presence or their advice. When the Indian army veteran Lieutenant Elliot warned Scarlett of the nature and the direction of the danger to his troops, Scarlett immediately paid heed to the warning and took Elliot's advice.

General Scarlett Deploys His Troops

Despite the huge Russian force on the hill threatening his men, General Scarlett turned his back to the enemy, faced his troops, and calmly prepared them for battle. Assisted by Elliot, Scarlett arranged his cavalry in tight, well-organized formations, as though they were about to take part in a military parade-ground display of horsemanship.

Suddenly Lord Lucan rode up. Furious at the sight before him, and fearful that once again the cavalry would not act, Lucan ordered Scarlett to attack. Someone blew the trumpet sound to move, but the order was ignored. Lord Lucan gave some verbal orders to the troops without conveying them to General Scarlett. These, too, were ignored.

The well-disciplined troops of the Heavy Brigade followed the directions given by their brigadier general. Scarlett continued, with almost complete disregard of Lucan, to bring his small force into satisfactory battle order before moving into action. According to historian Cecil Woodham-Smith, "To the watchers on the

Heights, the delay was all but unendurable" as Scarlett moved his men "a few feet this or that while the grey torrent of horsemen, appearing all the more irresistible for its deliberate measured pace" prepared for battle.

By the time Scarlett had completed the dressing of his troops, the wings of the Russian line had spread to their greatest extent. When Scarlett finally turned to face the Russians, he confronted a much longer line than had existed just moments before.

Charge of General Scarlett

But Scarlett had determined on a course of action. He did not change the disposition of his units. He had placed two squadrons of Scots Greys and one squadron of Inniskilling Dragoons in the first line, perhaps a total of three hundred men in all. The second line consisted only of the Fifth Dragoon Guards, the third contained the second Inniskilling squadron along with the Fourth Dragoon Guards and the Royals.

The first line of cavalry came to be known as Scarlett's Three Hundred. The Greys and the Inniskilling Dragoons had last fought together under Wellington against Napoleon. Their tradition of shared past glory made the men of the units eager to attack the enemy together. The Inniskillings in their scarlet jackets and helmets and the Greys with their famous bearskin headgear were easily seen and eagerly followed by the spectators on the hill behind them.

Scarlett's work was done. Although he could now have entrusted the charge to one of his subordinates, Scarlett was determined to lead his own men into action. He ordered his trumpeter to sound the charge. Then Scarlett, accompanied only

General Scarlett leads an enthusiastic cavalry against thousands of Russians in the Charge of the Heavy Brigade.

by Lieutenant Elliot, his trumpeter, and his orderly, a huge man named Shegog, set off to face the enemy. The four men rode fifty yards in front of the three hundred troops of the first line. Historian John Sweetman, presents a lively description of the general and his aide: "To the spectators on the Sapoune Ridge, the scene was pure theatre. Elliot in his cocked hat rode beside Scarlett, who wore a blue frocked coat and burnished helmet rather than a general's headdress."

The Russian gray mass waited on the hill above them. Scarlett, his sword thrust out, rode directly toward the center of the Russian forces to an officer who appeared to be the commander of the Russian cavalry.

To the spectators on the hill and to the front line of British troopers, the Russians, most of whom were still halted or at most riding at a walk, appeared to be shocked by the appearance of four horsemen, charging alone into the center of thousands of Russian cavalry.

Their appearance was so bewildering that the four British cavalrymen were able to cut down the Russian commanding officer, Major General Khaletski, who was severely wounded by Lieutenant Elliot's sword. General Scarlett drove his huge horse between the two nearest Russian troopers in the front line.

Although Scarlett was a bad swordsman and nearsighted, he kept his sword swinging through the air on both sides as he and his companions appeared to be enveloped by the huge Russian mass. Through violent slashings of their swords and the able maneuverings of their much larger and heavier horses, the four miraculously cut their way through the center of the Russian cavalry. The Russians were so closely packed that they were not able to use their weapons against the British.

Charge of the Greys and Inniskillings

Just as Scarlett momentarily disappeared from the view of the British onlookers on the heights, the Scots Greys and the Inniskilling Dragoons came charging into the Russian cavalry. Kinglake reports the event:

> They crashed in with a momentum so strong that no cavalry, extended in line and halted, could well have withstood the shock if it had been physically able to turn and fall back; but, whatever might be their inclination, the front-rank men of the Russian column were debarred from all means of breaking away to the rear by the weight of their own serried [in a serrated pattern] squadrons sloping up the hillside close behind them.

The Three Hundred, too, soon appeared to be swallowed up by the enemy. Observers from the Sapoune Heights saw only the tiny markings of the small British cavalry force, the red of the In-

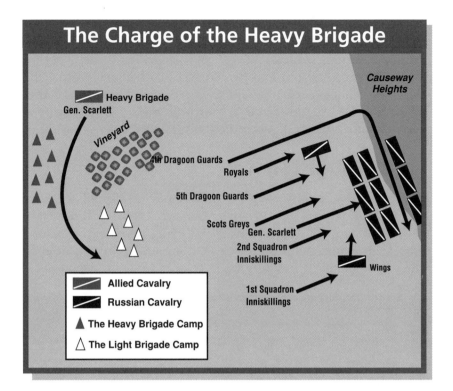

The Charge of the Heavy Brigade

Causeway Heights

Heavy Brigade
Gen. Scarlett

Vineyard

4th Dragoon Guards

Royals

5th Dragoon Guards

Scots Greys

Gen. Scarlett

2nd Squadron Inniskillings

Wings

1st Squadron Inniskillings

Allied Cavalry

Russian Cavalry

The Heavy Brigade Camp

The Light Brigade Camp

niskillings' scarlet coats and the high black bearskin hats of the Scots Greys in the great battle below them. From the distance they could hear the rumbles of battle and feared the worst had happened.

Suddenly a new movement of the Russian wings made it appear that Scarlett's valiant troops would be annihilated. "At the moment of impact," writes the historian the marquess of Anglesey, "the extended Russian wings began to close in from both flanks." It seemed to Lord Raglan and his staff that the Greys and Inniskillings were about to be destroyed front and rear by the crush of the Russians on the hill. A groan of despair rose from the group watching the scene from the hilltop.

Then, as all appeared to be lost, the Royals, the Fourth Dragoon Guards, the Fifth Dragoon Guards, and the last squadron of the Inniskillings charged against the Russians from four separate directions. In addition, contrary to their orders, as the historian Hibbert writes:

A few troops of the Light Brigade who had stolen away from their regiments charged in too, like uncontrollable school boys joining a pillow-fight, and finally two butchers dashed forward in their shirtsleeves, swinging swords as if they were meat-cleavers.

The Russian hussars who had swung in toward the center of their own line were attacked from the rear by the charging third line of the British cavalry. The shock tactics, especially effective against a stationary force, began to take their toll.

At the far side of the Russian mass, somehow General Scarlett emerged with only a few cuts. Elliot soon followed. He had received fourteen wounds, several of them to his head. If not for the stuffing he had put into his hat at the last minute before the battle, his skull probably would have received a fatal blow. After the action, he was described in the battle report as having been "only slightly wounded," according to historian Selby.

Battle Fought Fiercely

The end of the battle was violent and furious. In his old age General Ryzhov wrote: "In forty-two years of service and ten campaigns, among the Kulm, Leipzig and Paris, never before have I seen such action, with both sides cutting and thrusting at each other for so long." A British trooper, Temple Godman, reported:

As the situation seemed hopeless for the British, the Heavy Brigade launched an unexpected attack on the Russians' rear, turning the battle around.

All I saw were swords in the air in every direction, the pistols going off, and everyone hacking away right and left. In a moment the Greys were surrounded and hemmed completely in; there they were fighting back to back in the middle, the great bearskin caps high above the enemy.

British observers near Lord Raglan on the hill saw the great mass of men and horses locked in battle. Then they saw the gray mass begin to sway and then to break apart. The great mass of Russian horsemen appeared to shift, heave about, and finally turn and ride back up the hill to rejoin the remainder of the Russian army in the North Valley.

In only eight minutes, from 9:15 to 9:23 that morning, the action was over. The British were victorious. Against all canons of military practice, Scarlett and the Heavy Brigade, without infantry or artillery support, charged a force many times their strength that occupied the high ground of the battlefield. Despite the odds, they had driven the Russians from the hill.

The British did not take advantage of their victory. A few troopers of the Heavies did follow the fleeing Russians a short distance, but they were too disorganized after the furious battle to destroy the retreating enemy. The farther they moved from the South Valley, the more they fell under the fire of field guns the Russians had placed on the surrounding hills. General Scarlett sounded the recall of those members of the Heavy Brigade who still pursued the rear of the Russian cavalry.

Casualties

British casualties were remarkably light as a result of the Charge of the Heavy Brigade. Eight troopers were killed outright while some seventy others were wounded. The Russians lost about five hundred killed and wounded. Trooper Godman surveyed the South Valley the next day and reported:

> The ground was strewn with swords, broken and whole, trumpets, helmets, carbines etc., while a quantity of men were scattered all along as far as we had pursued. There must have been some forty or fifty of the enemy dead, besides wounded.

Since the British had lost their redoubts, the High Command was greatly relieved by the success of the Heavy Brigade. Lord Raglan sent General Scarlett a brief note of thanks: "Well done, the Heavy Brigade." Sir Colin Campbell rode up shouting, "Greys, gallant Greys! . . . I am sixty-one years old and if I were young again I should be proud to be in your ranks." A French general declared: "The victory of the Heavy Brigade was the most glorious thing I ever saw."

Bizarre Events Save the Life of a British Officer

Lieutenant Elliot played an extremely important role during the third phase of the Battle of Balaclava. Curiously his life was spared during the battle by a series of actions that he took prior to the battle. The historian Hibbert refers to a letter Elliot wrote in which he recounts these events:

> He had turned out that morning in a forage cap, explaining to General Scarlett that an Order now permitted it. "My staff shall be properly dressed." Elliot had gone back to his tent and found the chin strap of his cock-hat loose. He had begun to sew on a button when Scarlett called him out. He left the strap and stuffed a big silk handkerchief in the hat to make it tighter. It was to save his life.

During the charge of the Heavy Brigade, Elliot was struck in the head many times. The tightness of the fit of his hat, caused by the presence of the "unofficial" handkerchief, kept his hat in place and his skull intact.

Reaction of Lord Cardigan to Scarlett's Victory

Lord Cardigan, commander of the Light Brigade, appeared to be the only man not entirely pleased with the success of General Scarlett that day. During the charge, the Light Brigade behaved as onlookers. According to historian C. E. Vulliamy, when the Russians began to retreat, Major Morris "repeatedly urged the Brigadier to attack the rear of the Russian mass." Cardigan refused to take action.

Lord Cardigan claimed then and for the rest of his life that his orders were to remain where he was. In great frustration, however, during the battle, Lord Cardigan rode up and down his line muttering, "Damn those Heavies, they have the laugh on us this day." After the charge "he sat glumly on his horse . . . hearing the cheers and roars of the exulting British army." The historian Kinglake gathered this information from troopers who heard Lord Cardigan's remarks.

He deliberately took no action against the retreating Russian cavalry that passed almost directly across the front of his own line. Cardigan did not have what he considered specific orders to take action. He refused to put himself in a position in which he could be reprimanded by the much-hated Lord Lucan, his commanding officer. The Russian cavalrymen Cardigan thus permitted to escape soon took part in battle against the men of his own Light Brigade.

CHAPTER SEVEN

The Charge of the Light Brigade

Theirs not to reason why,
Theirs but to do and die:
Into the valley of Death
Rode the six hundred.

"The Charge of the Light Brigade"
Alfred, Lord Tennyson

A ll was quiet on the field of battle for about a half hour after the Russian cavalry retreated from the South Valley. The great mass of the Russian forces, about twenty-five thousand in all, formed an arc around three sides of the North Valley. There were six battalions of infantry, about thirty guns, and the cavalry, including those units that had fought against Campbell and then against Scarlett. The rear position of this great army brushed a line formed by an aqueduct and the Tchernaya River.

The Russian position at the end of the North Valley was well protected. A large number of infantry units and guns were in the hills to the east above the redoubts, and artillery units were also on the Fedioukine Heights, which lay to the north of the North Valley.

Despite this overwhelming strength, General Liprandi, as hesitant as his superiors, concluded that combat was over for the day. He did not even believe that the Russians would be able to hold the redoubts they had captured earlier in the morning. Therefore, Liprandi ordered the Odessa regiment to return to the redoubts with horses and ropes to carry off as trophies of war the British naval guns that the Turks left behind.

Meanwhile, the two British infantry divisions, the First under the duke of Cambridge and the Fourth under General Cathcart, slowly continued to descend from the Sapoune Heights on their way to the redoubts closest to the base of the Causeway Heights. Lord Raglan believed that the success of the Heavy Brigade made the recapture of the redoubts possible. The cavalry and infantry, acting in unison, should be able to regain these strategically important positions.

Raglan Sees Guns Being Dragged Away

The infantry moved too slowly to salvage the current situation, and Raglan made the fatal mistake of ordering the cavalry to undertake the action on its own.

Lord Raglan sent a message to Lord Lucan conveying his instructions: "Cavalry to advance and take advantage of any opportunity to recover the heights. They will be supported by the infantry which have been ordered to advance on two fronts." Lord Lucan was somewhat confused by the message. He did not understand that an opportunity currently presented itself for his cavalry to take action.

From where he stood at the base of the heights, Lucan could not see the enemy. The Russian cavalry force that Liprandi sent to remove the naval guns was hidden from his line of vision by the rise of the land before him. He did not know that the Russian cavalry was in the process of removing guns from the redoubts. He knew only about the presence of masses of enemy forces at the end of the North Valley. Equally important, the slow-moving British infantry divisions under the duke of Cambridge and General Cathcart were not in any position to support a cavalry action at that moment.

Nevertheless, from a strategic perspective now was the moment to strike. Todleben, in his account of the Crimean War, clearly makes this point:

> The capture of the redoubts seriously alarmed the Generals-in-Chief of the allied armies. By this feat of arms and the occupation by the Russians of the left bank of the Tchernaya at one and a quarter miles from Balaclava, the base of communication of the English was menaced. If the corps of General Liprandi had received some support that day, Balaclava would have fallen into our hands.

From the British perspective, the redoubts and the guns left behind by the Turks had to be retrieved, but Lord Lucan made no signs of movement.

Raglan, watching the action below, became frantic. From his vantage point he could see that the Russian cavalry was already removing the field guns. Why did Lucan not move? It was already forty-five minutes since Raglan had issued his last order. Was Lucan really a Lord Look-On, justifiably the butt of the jokes of many of the British junior officers?

Raglan issued yet another set of orders. These were written hastily in pencil on a scrap of brown paper by his quartermaster general, Sir Richard Airey:

> Lord Raglan wishes the cavalry to advance rapidly to the front—follow the enemy and try to prevent the enemy carrying away the guns—Troops Horse Artillery may accompany—French cavalry is on our left—Immediate.

The order was handed to Captain Lewis Edward Nolan, Airey's aide-de-camp, and one of the best horsemen in the army. He was to deliver the urgent message directly to Lord Lucan.

Captain Nolan

Captain Nolan was an extremely well regarded career soldier who had written extensively on the art of horsemanship. Certainly William Howard Russell, the *Times* reporter, held him in high esteem:

> A braver soldier than Captain Nolan the army did not possess. He was known to all his arm of the service for his entire devotion to his profession, and his name must be familiar to all who take interest in our cavalry for his excellent work, published a year ago, on our drill and system of remount and breaking horses.

Unfortunately, Nolan was the wrong messenger to send to the sensitive earl of Lucan. Because of his own jealous nature, Lord Lucan would see Nolan as a threat and would have a difficult time

The original order from Lord Raglan that set the Charge of the Light Brigade in motion.

Captain Lewis Edward Nolan

Captain Lewis Edward Nolan was one of the most capable of the British officers to serve in the Crimean War. He was a cavalryman of great experience and intelligence. His book on cavalry tactics and the training of horses was widely used among European armies. Nolan was part of the staff attached to Lord Raglan, the overall commander of the British forces, but his views on the proper use of the cavalry were disregarded by Lord Lucan, the cavalry general, largely because of Nolan's association with the army in India. In Lucan's mind, any officer who had to earn his living by having become a professional soldier was not worthy of Lucan's consideration.

Nolan regarded Lord Lucan and Lord Cardigan as egotistical bunglers. He was furious at the failure of the cavalry generals to take action in the field against the Russians, and it was Nolan who coined the term "Lord Look-On" to describe Lord Lucan; the nickname soon spread through the entire British army.

Nolan knew that Lord Raglan wanted to protect the guns on the redoubts, not the guns at the far end of the North Valley. Lord Raglan sent Nolan to deliver that order to Lord Lucan on October 25, 1854, but the lack of clarity in Raglan's written message to Lord Lucan and Nolan's inability to make clear the exact nature of Lord Raglan's order led indirectly to Nolan's own untimely death and the ill-fated Charge of the Light Brigade.

Captain Lewis Edward Nolan delivered the order that resulted in the Charge of the Light Brigade and, ultimately, Nolan's own death.

acting in a civil manner toward him. Lucan could scarcely discuss with Nolan the meaning of Lord Raglan's unclear order or the proper course of action to take in executing it.

Standing at Lord Raglan's side on the heights, Nolan had watched with horror as the Russians prepared to remove the guns from the redoubts. He was anxious to take Raglan's message down to the British cavalry camp. The last words Nolan heard from Raglan were: "Tell Lucan to attack immediately." Nolan then mounted his horse and plunged recklessly and directly down the steep slope of the Sapoune Heights and arrived at Lucan's headquarters in only a few moments. He was out of breath and full of fury that Lucan, whom he personally despised, had ignored the earlier message to move against the Odessa regiment.

In letters to friends in England, Nolan had referred to Lucan as the cautious ass and Cardigan as the dangerous ass. Tragically, the events of the day would underline the accuracy of his evaluation of the cavalry leaders. On that late October morning, Nolan feared that the cautious ass would lose the opportunity to retake the redoubts.

Nolan handed Lord Raglan's orders to General Lucan. What the historian Cecil Woodham-Smith calls an "unseemly squabble" now took place between these angry men, that is,

> between a subordinate officer and a lieutenant general. Both of them had lost their tempers; Lucan because of the absurdity and ambiguity of the order [Lucan believed Raglan wanted him to attack the guns at the end of the North Valley], Nolan because of Lucan's hesitation. [Nolan knew Raglan wanted Lucan to attack the Russians removing the guns from the redoubts.]

Lord Lucan Reluctant to Follow Orders from Raglan

The general slowly read the words on the brown slip of paper. He turned to Nolan and furiously asked: "Attack, sir? Attack what? What guns, sir?"

Nolan became infuriated by Lucan's questioning of Lord Raglan's orders and by his failure to comply with the earlier ones. With a reckless wave of his hand in what he probably thought was the direction of the Causeway Heights, Nolan shouted back, "There, my lord, is your enemy! There are your guns!"

Lord Lucan did not ask any further questions of the insubordinate captain. Instead he rode slowly toward Lord Cardigan. Cardigan and the Light Brigade had stood almost motionless when the Heavy Brigade under General Scarlett scored a magnificent victory over the Russian cavalry. The young men of the Light Brigade and their lordly brigadier general were eager for the same glory.

In fact, by midmorning Lord Cardigan was jealous of the magnificence of the Heavies' performance. Cardigan's jealousy and his own lack of military experience boded tragically for the troopers under his command, but the troopers themselves were anxious to go into battle and prove their worth. They would follow Lord Cardigan wherever and whenever he ordered them to attack. These facts would lead to a massive tragedy.

Lord Lucan showed his brother-in-law the orders that he had just received from Captain Nolan. In addition, Lucan told Cardigan that Cardigan was to "advance steadily and keep your men well in hand."

Cardigan Questions Orders

Lord Cardigan read the message. Like Lord Lucan, Cardigan was perplexed. Even with his limited military experience, Cardigan understood, as Russell explained to his readers: "It is a maxim of war, that a cavalry never acts without support and infantry should be close at hand when cavalry carry guns, as the effect is only instantaneous."

Lord Cardigan tried to argue with his brother-in-law. "Certainly, sir," he told Lord Lucan, "but allow me to point out to you that the Russians have a battery in the valley in our front, and batteries and riflemen on each flank."

Lord Lucan replied, "I cannot help that. It is Lord Raglan's positive order that the Light Brigade attacks immediately."

Both Lord Lucan and Lord Cardigan believed that Raglan had ordered the Light Brigade, unaided by infantry support, to charge down the valley flanked on both sides by enemy guns and capture the mass of Russian guns at its far end. It occurred to neither of them that the order referred to the guns abandoned by the Turks in the redoubts. Neither man sought an explanation from Captain Nolan, waiting only several paces away and the only man who knew exactly what Lord Raglan intended them to do.

After this exchange with his commanding officer, Lord Cardigan determined to carry out his orders to the last detail. Lord Cardigan was the last male in his family, and he believed that Raglan's order would result in his own death. Cardigan turned and muttered to Lord George Paget, "Well, here goes the last of the Brudenelles [his family name]."

He placed himself ten yards ahead of the Light Brigade. The men of the brigade looked glorious that day in their blue- and cherry-colored uniforms with gold trimmings across the chest and shoulders. They made perfect targets in the bright October late-morning sunlight.

Charge of the Light Brigade

At 11:00 A.M. Lord Cardigan set off to attack the Russian gun emplacements without any signal by trumpet or voice. He increased his speed from trot to canter to gallop to full charge with the Light Brigade following. Behind Cardigan 673 men and horses advanced down the valley. They were arranged in three lines: in the first the Thirteenth Light Dragoons and the Seventeenth Lancers; in the second line only the Eleventh Hussars; and in the third line the Fourth Light Dragoons and the Eighth Hussars. "Folly it was indeed; heroic folly; superb discipline under the orders of incurable stupidity; a sight moving men to tears, laughter, rage and admiration," wrote the historian Cecil Woodham-Smith.

The Light Brigade was followed at some distance by Lord Lucan, who decided to lead the Heavy Brigade himself. Shortly, however, the two became separated because of the difference in the speed at which they rode. When Lord Lucan saw the men of the Light Brigade begin to fall under the deadly fire from the Russian guns on the surrounding hills, he slowed his pace.

British troopers and horses lay dead and dying long before the Light Brigade reached the Russian guns. Soon some of Lucan's own Royals and Greys came under cross fire from the enemy batteries to the right and left of the valley. Lucan then understood the scope of the horrible mistake in judgment in which he had just participated.

Not acknowledging publicly his own role in the decision to attack, Lucan announced to Lord William Paulett, who rode beside him: "They have sacrificed the Light Brigade; they shall not the Heavy, if I can help it." Lord Lucan decided he could only assist the Light Brigade by protecting it against pursuit if and when it returned back to its camp. Thus, the Heavy Brigade did not take part in the attack on the Russian guns at the end of "the valley of death."

Meanwhile, Captain Nolan, who had asked permission to join the charge, realized almost immediately that a tragic misunderstanding had occurred. Cardigan was leading his men in the wrong direction. Instead of heading for the Causeway Heights, Cardigan was leading his men against massed guns at the far end of the North Valley.

Death of Captain Nolan

Nolan immediately left his place in line. He galloped across the front line of charging cavalrymen and then in front of Cardigan with his sword pointing in the direction of the Causeway Heights. According to historian C. E. Vulliamy, Nolan "obviously was trying to change the direction of the Brigadier, to make him wheel out of the valley."

Nolan's warning came too late. The Light Brigade was almost immediately under attack by both the batteries on the Fedioukine Heights to the left and the guns on the Causeway Heights to the right. The Light Brigade was riding to its doom down a deadly gauntlet with still more deadly guns belching out death at the end of the North Valley.

Nolan was the very first victim of the merciless onslaught. A bullet struck him in the heart almost immediately. His horse turned around and rode back through the on-galloping Light Brigade. Although he was dead, a "fearful cry" continued to emerge from his body. He rode with his sword held high and erect in the saddle as his horse carried him almost to the point from which the Light Brigade had begun its ride before his dead body fell to the ground.

British and French officers on the Sapoune Heights realized that there had been a terrible misunderstanding. "Cardigan must have lost his head," one British general announced. General Bosquet declared that what they were seeing was "Magnificent, but not war," adding a sentence that tactful historians rarely quote—"It is madness."

Even the Russians could not understand the complete lack of military judgment that brought the virtually defenseless Light Brigade charging directly into the blazing mouths of the Russian batteries. At first General Liprandi thought the soldiers had been moved to charge because they were all drunk. Later he learned

The Light Brigade charges in the wrong direction, heading straight into the massed Russian guns.

Captain Nolan, his dead body still riding his horse, continues through the Light Brigade he tried to warn.

from captured British troopers that this was not true. They told Liprandi that they had not even eaten breakfast, and their haversacks contained untouched rations of rum. "You are noble fellows," Liprandi told a group of prisoners, "and I am sincerely sorry for you."

Meanwhile, more and more men and horses were struck by the deadly Russian cross fire as they continued their wild ride down the gauntlet. Soon riderless horses and horseless men were seen on the plain. This added confusion and increasing horror to the terrible error.

Yet onward rode the Light Brigade with Lord Cardigan on his charger, Ronald, leading the way. Cardigan looked neither to the right nor to the left. He continued the mad charge until he actually

Lord Cardigan leaps over Russian artillery while charging back to camp. The irresponsible Cardigan disregarded the welfare of his troops as he raced to lodge a complaint against the fallen Captain Nolan.

reached the Russian guns at the far end of the valley. He rode through the ranks of Russian artillerymen manning their field guns.

Belatedly the Don Cossacks, horsemen from the Don River region in Russia, stationed far behind the guns realized that the English horsemen were heading directly toward them. General Ryzhov tried hurriedly to bring up the cavalry to protect the battery, but he was too late. The handful of British dragoons and lancers from the first line who made it to the battery began slashing at the Russians with their sabers and destroyed some of the guns that the Russian artillerymen were desperately trying to drag away.

Meanwhile Lord Cardigan rode beyond the Russian battery against Ryzhov's chestnut-colored charger but did not harm him. Cardigan then turned, evaded several attempts by the Cossack cavalry to capture him, and returned up the valley. He never stopped to ascertain the fate of his troops as the second and third lines crashed into the waiting Russian army.

Cardigan's Anger at Nolan

The most important thing on Cardigan's mind was not the disaster to his men but how quickly he could return to camp "to lodge a complaint about the infamous conduct of Captain Nolan." When he met General Scarlett upon his return, he complained that contrary to all military norms, Nolan had tried to ride in front of him. Ironically, the two men met almost at the exact spot where Nolan had fallen to the ground. General Scarlett with great sadness and much anger told Lord Cardigan that "he had just ridden over Nolan's body."

While this exchange took place, the remaining 50 British troopers of the original 270 of the first line got to the Russian guns and made them inoperable. The rest of the British were shot down or had their horses shot from under them. Finally, only 30 survivors of the front line, apart from Cardigan who actually entered the Russian battery, remained to fight their way back to their camp.

The surviving British cavalry of the other two lines soon also found themselves behind enemy lines. They now faced the massed Russian infantry units that Liprandi had held in reserve. Two remnants of the Light Brigade rallied behind Lord George Paget and Colonel Edward Shewell. These men then turned and fought their way back up the North Valley, which was a shambles. What they saw were "dead horses, dead and wounded men, riderless terrified horses with Russian guns and riflemen on the Heights" continuing to fire on the pathetic remnants of the once proud Light Brigade.

The ruined remains of the Light Brigade continued to drag themselves back to camp throughout the afternoon. Their once beautiful uniforms were torn and covered with blood. Many dragged along "beloved horses limping and bleeding to death behind them." Some troopers limped back in pairs, supporting one another in their attempts to regain camp before they were killed by the Russian cavalry that made attempts to reach them.

That even this handful escaped death was partly because of assistance from the French. Under General D'Allenville, the Fourth Regiment of Chasseurs d'Afrique, about two hundred men, attacked the Russian guns on the Fedioukine Heights. The guns

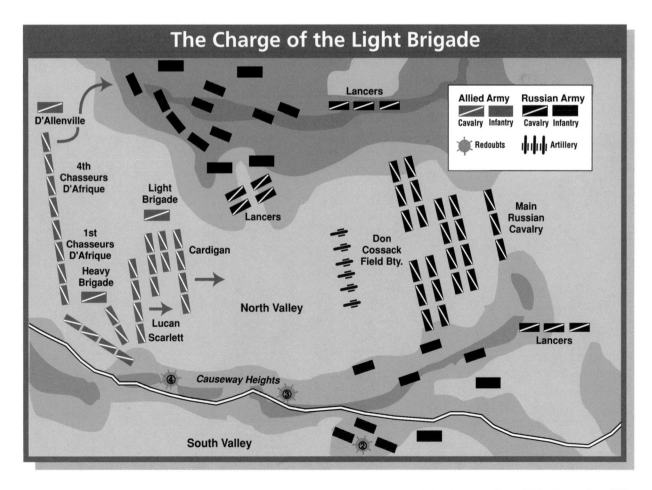

Hideous Carnage During the Charge of the Light Brigade

The following accounts, taken from diaries of men who rode with Lord Cardigan, provide graphic descriptions of the horrors of the Charge of the Light Brigade.

Before they had broken into the charge, the right-hand man of the 17th, old John Lee, was all but smashed by a shell; he gave Wightman's arm a switch (touched it with his crop), as with a strange smile he quickly said, "Domino!" and fell out of his saddle. His old grey mare kept alongside for some distance, treading on and tearing out her entrails as she galloped, til at length she dropped with a strange shriek.

Peter Marsh was Wightman's left-hand man, and next beyond him was Private Dudley. The explosion of a shell had swept down four men on Dudley's left, and Wightman heard him ask Marsh if he had noted what a hole "that bloody shell had made" on his left front. "Hold your foul-mouthed tongue," answered Peter. "Swearing like a blackguard when you may be knocked into eternity the next minute!"

Just then Wightman got a musket bullet through his right knee and another in the shin and his horse got three bullet wounds in his neck. Man and horse were bleeding so fast that Marsh begged him to fall out. But he would not, pointing out that in a few minutes they would be into them. Instead, he sent his spurs well home and faced it to be with his comrades. It was about this time that Sergeant Talbot had his head clean carried off by a round shot, yet for another thirty yards farther the headless body kept in the saddle, the lance at the charge firmly gripped under the right arm.

British soldiers continue the battle that will later result in a deadly, gory defeat.

had rained deadly fire on the left flank of the Light Brigade during its charge down the valley. The chasseurs were able to cut down General Jaboritsky's guns and to overrun the Russian battery, but the French could not take the guns from their positions without support. In this action, the French lost two captains and fifty killed and wounded. They remained on the heights long enough to protect the British remnant that straggled back to camp, fired on now only by the guns from the south.

The entire action—the charge down the valley, the hideous slaughter, and the return—took less than twenty minutes. Two hundred and forty-seven men were missing from the ranks when the roll call was taken. Many others later died of their wounds. In addition, 475 horses were either killed outright or were soon shot by the farriers, men who combined veterinary surgery with horseshoeing, who put the most gravely wounded animals out of their misery. The Russians lost 238 killed and another 312 badly wounded.

Cardigan Tries to Explain His Actions

Lord Raglan asked Lord Cardigan what had happened. "My Lord, I hope you will not blame me, for I received the order to attack from my superior officer in front of the troops." With that explanation Lord Cardigan took himself off to his yacht for a warm meal prepared by his French chef.

Lord Raglan reviewed the remains of the Light Brigade later that afternoon. He was informed that of the 673 men who began the charge, only 195 were fit for action six hours later. "You have lost the Light Brigade!" was all that Raglan said icily to Lucan when they met that afternoon.

Some of the survivors of the four actions that day recovered from their wounds and exertions and prepared to undertake the defenses of other British positions between Balaclava and the port of Sebastopol. Others, already weakened by disease, died of malnutrition and medical neglect. Shortly after the Battle of Balaclava, both Lord Lucan and Lord Cardigan returned to England to defend what remained of their military reputations.

A few of the gallant cavalry horses survived to return to England. Sergeant Mitchell, who served under William Paget, knew of one wounded horse that went through the rest of the campaign, returned to England, and was still appearing regularly on parade until 1862. Ronald, valiant horse of Lord Cardigan, survived the Charge of the Light Brigade unscathed. He returned to England with his master, lived a long life, and even outlived the earl of Cardigan by several years.

CHAPTER EIGHT

Conclusions

Finest thing ever attempted.

Lord Raglan

Some battles are decisive. The British surrender at the Battle of Saratoga in 1778 brought the French into the war on the side of the American army and assured that the colonies would successfully gain independence from Great Britain. The British victory under Admiral Horatio Nelson at the Battle of Trafalgar in 1805 made it impossible for the French under Napoleon Bonaparte to invade England. The success of the Allied armies during the Battle of Normandy assured them a firm toehold in Nazi-dominated Europe and the promise of ultimate success against Germany in World War II.

The Battle of Balaclava was not one of these decisive historic battles. Despite the heroic stands of the Turks and of the Highlanders under Sir Colin Campbell, the valor of the Heavy Brigade under General Scarlett, and the foolish heroism and ultimate destruction of the Light Brigade, nothing significant was accomplished that day except mass carnage.

The British and French had hoped for a short war, a rapid assault on Sebastopol, and the withdrawal of their troops before the onset of winter. The Russians wanted to capture Balaclava and drive Britain out of the war. None of these hopes was realized. Instead the British and French continued their siege of Sebastopol. The Russians continued to resist the allies' efforts to break down the resistance of the defenders of the Russian naval base.

Lack of decisive victory that day for one side or the other helped to ensure that the war continued for almost another two years. As Trooper Lysons expressed so clearly in a letter to his mother:

Now we are prisoners in the little bit of ground we are encamped on; nothing to do, no change, no amusement, no books, only now and then a mail. However, I pray God better times will come some day. Anything like common comfort would indeed appear sweet now. To be clean and get things on, oh, what a luxury it would be!

Trench warfare before Sebastopol became the chief occupation of the allies and their destruction the main preoccupation of the Russians. Technicians developed new weapons of destruction. The longer the war continued, the more difficult it became to make concessions leading to a peace settlement that would not create long-term animosities. By the time the conflict finally ended, some of the basic civility that had enabled the European powers to work together since the end of the Napoleonic wars had disappeared.

The allies care for their wounded soldiers in the aftermath of the war. The Battle of Balaclava resulted in devastating losses, a drawn-out war, and animosity between nations.

The battle did bring about some changes in the disposition of the opposing armies around Balaclava. The British lost the outer perimeter of their defense system when the Russians gained control of the Causeway Heights and the road that ran along its summit. The Russians continued their hold on several of the redoubts and increased the number of their troops committed to the defense of those positions. They also increased their strength on the Fedioukine Heights, and as a result they dominated the whole plain of Balaclava.

The British in turn committed additional troops to their posts on the heights overlooking the port from the Baidar Valley side of the harbor from where the marines had assisted General Campbell. The French provided some minor troop support to assist the British in holding their now-reduced defensive perimeter around the harbor. It also became increasingly clear that the reduced size of the British force meant that the French would play a dominant role in the Crimean War.

Since the British defensive perimeter became so narrow after the battle, for a time the High Command even considered abandoning Balaclava entirely and establishing a new port for British supply ships. In the end Raglan decided to remain.

As a result, the British army on the Chersonese Heights, which overlooked Sebastopol, had to bring up their supplies from Balaclava on the narrow, unpaved road leading from the harbor. The Russians continued their hold on the more modern Woronzov Road.

As winter set in and the unpaved road became difficult to traverse, the amount of supplies that could be hauled up the road dramatically decreased. The British troops in the trenches before Sebastopol and the animals that hauled their supplies suffered terribly during the winter months. The loss of life was appalling. The following spring the British rectified the situation by building a short military railroad line leading from the harbor to the heights.

From a military perspective, the Battle of Balaclava demonstrated to the Russian High Command that the British cavalry units were heroic beyond measure. During the remainder of the war the Russian cavalry remained wary of the few remaining British troops and took every opportunity to avoid engaging them in battle.

Despite the respect Menshikov's forces now accorded the British cavalry, the Russian commander concluded that the British were far weaker than he had anticipated after the Russian defeat at the Alma in September 1854.

The Russians brought the captured British guns back to Sebastopol along with the captured Turkish standard. The Russians' spirits were lifted by these symbols of military triumph. Todleben noted that after the Battle of Balaclava:

The catastrophe of the Alma was forgotten; unlimited confidence was again placed in the superiority of Russian arms and the moral tone of the garrison being completely restored, it returned to the display of the greatest energy.

General Menshikov was particularly pleased by the Battle of Balaclava, which seemingly restored the reputation he had tarnished at the Alma. Menshikov decided to continue his own offensive. This led him to undertake a large, inconclusive skirmish the very next day. Then on November 5, the Russians launched the Battle of Inkerman in which thousands of Russian and British soldiers died in a nearly successful Russian effort to force the British off the Inkerman Heights.

Yet the Russians did not learn the valuable lessons they might have garnered from the Battle of Balaclava. The Russian High Command suffered by forbidding individual commanders to display any initiative and by being unwilling to change its plans to fit altered situations. The Russians continued to rely on the use of masses of men rather than on the skillful use of those men.

Sir George Cathcart leads his division in the Battle of Inkerman, an attempt by the Russians to drive the British off the Inkerman Heights.

These practices did not change. The Russians continued to send their troops in massed columns throughout the remainder of the war. Thousands of Russian soldiers were used as cannon fodder and died because their replacements were easily obtained.

The British High Command did not assimilate and adapt to what it had learned during the Battle of Balaclava. The leaders failed to appreciate the great efforts and sustaining power demonstrated by their Turkish allies in the opening moments of the battle. The officers tended to discount Turkish reconnaissance information, and allied troops often abused Turkish soldiers for the remainder of the war.

The British army continued to rely on the use of officers who obtained their commissions through purchase rather than on professional soldiers who were skilled and trained. Despite the superior service provided by professional soldiers such as Campbell, Elliot, Nolan, and others at Balaclava, British society was not ready to abandon the tradition of leadership by virtue of high birth. The army certainly was not ready to clean its own house.

On the other hand, the Battle of Balaclava was the opening salvo in the campaign to end this inefficient and wasteful method of providing officers for the army. For the first time British newsmen observed and freely and honestly described the ineptitude of the officers who led the British army. People in England

A bleak, rubble-filled cemetery on Cathcart's Hill captures the essence of the Crimean War, in which both sides suffered heavy losses and failed to learn from their tragic mistakes.

learned about the details of the Battle of Balaclava, including the magnificent but unnecessary destruction of the Light Brigade and the foolish, ultimately deadly behaviors of Lords Lucan and Cardigan. They read about the lack of coordination among the branches of the military and the cruel and thoughtless manner in which many officers treated their soldiers.

The many reports written by William Russell and other journalists, which appeared regularly in the *Times*, exposed the ineptitude of an archaic military system. The English population avidly read these reports, and for the first time in the history of warfare, civilians learned about the fate of the fathers, sons, and brothers who went off to war.

The reports of the Battle of Balaclava provided the first of a series of dramatic revelations on the state of the army. They caused anger, disgust, and finally shame at the treatment accorded British soldiers and the failure of their leaders to lead. Ultimately, after long and tedious legislative battles, these revelations led to the reform of the British army.

For Further Reading

Peter Gibbs, *Crimean Blunder*. London: Frederick Muller, 1960. Written by an Englishman who argues that the actors and actions of the Crimean War were foolish in the extreme. Gibbs contends that the war could easily have been avoided if thoughtful and capable leaders had been in charge of the governments of England, France, and Russia in 1854.

Constantin de Grunwald, *Tzar Nicholas I*. New York: Macmillan, 1955. Short account of the reign of Nicholas I that provides insights regarding the war from a Russian perspective.

Christopher Hibbert, *The Destruction of Lord Raglan: A Tragedy of the Crimean War, 1854–1855*. London: Longmans, 1961. An extremely sympathetic account of Lord Raglan's role in the Crimean campaign. The British leader is portrayed as a thoughtful, hardworking, misunderstood man whose failures in the Crimea were as much the fault of an unreformed, out-of-date military system as they were of his own leadership.

A. W. Kinglake, *The Invasion of the Crimea: Its Origins and an Account of Its Progress Down to the Death of Lord Raglan*. London: William Blackwood and Sons, 1877. Written by a war correspondent in the Crimea who was critical of Lord Raglan and his leadership of the war effort, but tried to explain away some of this criticism by demonstrating that the entire British military was even more at fault than was the commander in the field. One of the most important accounts of the events of the Crimean War.

William Howard Russell, *General Todleben's History of the Defense of Sebastopol, 1854–5: A Review*. London: Tinsley Brothers, 1865. Russell translated and edited the Russian general's account of events and added his own commentary regarding the validity of Todleben's interpretation.

William Howard Russell, *The War: From the Landing at Gallipoli to the Death of Lord Raglan*. London: George Routledge, 1855. Contains the letters that W. H. Russell, correspondent for the *Times* of London, sent to his newspaper editor. Russell's reports alerted the British government and population to the horrors that the British army experienced in the Crimea.

John Selby, *The Thin Red Line of Balaclava*. London: Hamish Hamilton, 1970. Account based on the diaries of participants in the war and filled with colorful and poignant details of the bravery, heroism, and individual suffering of both men and animals.

Anthony Sterling, *The Story of the Highland Brigade in the Crimea*. London: Hastings House, 1895. Wonderful details of the actions involving the Ninety-third Highland Regiment. The volume is based on letters that this soldier wrote between 1854 and 1856.

John Sweetman, *Balaclava: 1854*. London: Osprey Publishing, 1990. Contains extremely useful maps depicting the disposition of the British and Russian armies on October 25, l854.

Cecil Woodham-Smith, *The Reason Why*. New York: McGraw-Hill, 1960. Wonderfully rich, colorful account of one of history's most famous cavalry charges. Book is full of details regarding the personalities of the British military leaders whose dislike of each other led to the destruction of the Light Brigade.

Additional Works Consulted

Marquess of Anglesey, ed., *'Little Hodge' Being Extracts from the Diaries and Letters of Colonel Edward Cooper Hodge Written During the Crimean War, 1854–1856*. London: Leo Cooper, 1971. Wonderful diary written by a cavalry officer that covers the entire two years of the war as seen from the muddy trenches.

John Black Atkins, *The Life of Sir William Howard Russell*. Vol. 1. London: John Murray, 1911. Contains much useful information regarding the role played by the first special correspondent of the *Times* of London in making people in England understand the horrors associated with the Crimean War.

Diplomatic Study on the Crimean War (1852–1856). Vol. 1. Russian Official Publication. London: W. H. Allen, 1882. Contains information pertaining to the position of the Russian government in the negotiations among the European powers whose interests in Turkey were being threatened.

George Palmer Evelyn, *A Diary of the Crimea*. London: Gerald Duckworth, 1954. Account by a soldier who participated in the Crimean War. It is filled with details of the suffering of the British troops.

Archibald Forbes, *The Life of Napoleon the Third*. New York: Dodd, Mead, 1897. Provides useful information, placing the Crimean War within the context of Napoleon's overall foreign policy.

David M. Goldfrank, *The Origins of the Crimean War*. London: Longman, 1994. Account of the political background to the crisis that preceded the Crimean War.

Edward Hamley, *The War in the Crimea*. London: Seeley, 1910. Very readable account of the events leading up to and associated with the Crimean War from the perspective of an English officer.

Blanchard Jerrold, *The Life of Napleon III*. Vol. 4. London: Longmans, Green, 1882. Old-fashioned account of the life of Napoleon III, based on state records and personal accounts by his contemporaries. Sheds some interesting light on French involvement in the Crimean War.

Andrew D. Lambert, *The Crimean War: British Grand Strategy, 1853–56*. Manchester: Manchester University Press, 1990. Describes the Crimean War as a worldwide conflict, involving not only events in the Black Sea but also events in the Pacific Ocean, the Baltic Sea, and in Asia.

W. Bruce Lincoln, *Nicholas I, Emperor and Autocrat of All the Russias*. Bloomington: Indiana University Press, 1980. Describes the inflexibility of the tsar and the system he created and suggests that this inflexibility and the regimentation of a backward country contributed to the loss in the Crimean War.

Daniel Lysons, *The Crimean War from First to Last*. London: John Murray, 1895. Delightful series of letters from a general officer to his family in London, showing growing disgust with the lack of insight and planning for the British army in the Crimea.

B. Kingsley Martin, *The Triumph of Lord Palmerston*. London: George Allen & Unwin, 1924. A study of public opinion in England that led to that country's decision to assist Turkey in 1854.

Alan Warwick Palmer, *The Banner of Battle: The Story of the Crimean War*. New York: St. Martin's Press, 1987. Account of Crimean War from the perspective of recent understanding of the relationships among the belligerents in the mid-1850s.

Albert Seaton, *The Crimean War, a Russian Chronicle*. New York: St. Martin's Press, 1977. Discusses the origins and events of the Crimean War from the perspective of the tsar of Russia and the military and political leaders of the tsar's government.

Harold Temperley, *England and the Near East*. London: Longmans, Green, 1936. Extremely detailed account of the diplomatic exchanges that led to the outbreak of the Crimean War.

Evelyn E. P. Tisdall, *Restless Consort*. London: Stanley Paul, 1952. Readable account of the role that Albert, the prince consort, played in English affairs during this period.

Alexis S. Troubetzkoy, *The Road to Balaklava*. Toronto: Trafalgar Press, 1986. Describes the many accidents and misunderstandings among the political leaders that led to the Crimean War.

Philip Warner, *The Fields of War: A Young Cavalryman's Crimean Campaign*. London: John Murray, 1977. Edited review of the letters of Temple Godman, a cavalry officer who survived the entire Crimean campaign and wrote letters to his family describing his experiences.

David Wetzel, *The Crimean War: A Diplomatic History*. New York: Columbia University Press, 1985. Sketches the involvement of the major European diplomatic leaders in the crisis in Turkey and their inability to find a way to avoid war.

C. E. Vulliamy, *Crimea: The Campaign of 1854–1856*. London: Jonathan Cape, 1939. Well-balanced account that updates earlier descriptions by participants in the Crimean War.

Index

Picture Credits

Cover photo: The Bettmann Archive

The Bettman Archive, 29

Corbis-Bettmann, 12, 99

The Hulton-Deutsch Collection, 8 (both), 17, 18, 20, 21 (top), 24, 25, 27, 32, 43, 44, 47, 49, 54, 59, 63, 66, 68, 69, 77, 94, 101, 102

Peter Newark's Historical Pictures, 93

Peter Newark's Military Pictures, 11, 15, 21 (bottom), 37, 38, 41, 72, 73, 79, 82, 87, 88, 92, 96

About the Author

Deborah Bachrach was born and raised in New York City, where she received her undergraduate education. She earned a Ph.D. in history from the University of Minnesota. Dr. Bachrach has taught at the University of Minnesota as well as at St. Francis College, Joliet, Illinois, and Queens College, the City University of New York. In addition, she has worked for many years in the fields of medical research and public policy development.